Measuring: From Paces to Feet

A unit of study for grades 3–4
from USED NUMBERS: REAL DATA IN THE CLASSROOM

Developed at Technical Education Research Centers and Lesley College

Rebecca B. Corwin and Susan Jo Russell

7710

DALE SEYMOUR PUBLICATIONS

The *Used Numbers* materials were prepared with the support of National Science Foundation Grant No. MDR-8651649. Any opinions, findings, conclusions, or recommendations expressed in this publication are those of the authors and do not necessarily represent the views of the National Science Foundation. These materials shall be subject to a royalty-free, irrevocable, worldwide, nonexclusive license in the United States Government to reproduce, perform, translate, and otherwise use and to authorize others to use such materials for Government purposes.

Cover design and illustrations: Rachel Gage

Order number DS01025
ISBN 0-86651-503-8

DALE
SEYMOUR
PUBLICATIONS
P.O. BOX 10888
PALO ALTO, CA 94303

4 5 6 7 8 9 10 11 12-MA-96 95 94 93

USED NUMBERS STAFF

Co-principal investigators

Susan Jo Russell
Technical Education Research Centers (TERC)

Susan N. Friel
Lesley College

Curriculum development

Rebecca B. Corwin (TERC and Lesley College)
Tim Barclay (TERC)
Antonia Stone (Playing to Win)

Research and evaluation

Janice R. Mokros (TERC)
Alana Parkes (TERC)
Debra Gustafson (TERC)
John Olive (University of Georgia)
Deborah Ruff (University of Georgia)
Heide Wiegel (University of Georgia)
Bonnie Brownstein (Institute for Schools of the Future)
Ellen Bialo (Institute for Schools of the Future)
Michele Arsenault (Institute for Schools of the Future)
Mary Fullmer (University of Chicago)

Design and production

Elisabeth Roberts (TERC)
Jessica Goldberg (TERC)
LeAnn Davis (TERC)
John Abbe (TERC)
Laurie Aragon (COMAP)

Cooperating classrooms for this unit

Eric Johnson
Boston Public Schools

Connie Brady
New York City Public Schools

Laurie Friedlander
New York City Public Schools

Dolly Davis
Clarke County Public Schools, Georgia

Jane Holman
Clarke County Public Schools, Georgia

Advisory board

Joan Akers, California State Department of Education
Bonnie Brownstein, Institute for Schools of the Future
James Landwehr, AT&T Bell Laboratories
Steven Leinwand, Connecticut State Department of Education
John Olive, University of Georgia
David Pillemer, Wellesley College
Andee Rubin, Bolt Beranek and Newman Laboratories
Cindy Stephens, D. C. Heath
Marion Walter, University of Oregon
Virginia Wooley, Boston Museum of Science

Thanks also to advice and comment from Marilyn Burns, Solomon A. Garfunkel (COMAP), and Bob Willcutt.

CONTENTS

PREFACE

In an information-rich society such as ours, statistics are an increasingly important aspect of daily life. We are constantly bombarded with information about everything around us. This wealth of data can become confusing, or it can help us make choices about our actions.

Educators and mathematicians now stress the importance of incorporating data analysis and statistics into the elementary mathematics curriculum to prepare students for living and working in a world filled with information based on data. The *Curriculum and Evaluation Standards for School Mathematics*, published by the National Council of Teachers of Mathematics in 1989, highlights statistics as one of the key content strands for all grade levels.

Many teachers see the need to support students in becoming better problem solvers in mathematics. However, it is difficult to find problems that give students the kind of experiences they need, are manageable in the classroom, and lead to the learning of essential mathematics. The area of data analysis—collecting, organizing, graphing, and interpreting data—provides a feasible, engaging context in which elementary grade students can do real mathematics. Students of all ages are interested in real data about themselves and the world around them.

Teaching statistics: Pedagogical issues

We introduce students to good literature in their early years. We do not reserve great literature until they are older—on the contrary, we encourage them to read it or we read it to them. Similarly, we can give young students experience with real mathematical processes rather than save the good mathematics for later.

Through collecting and analyzing real data, students encounter the uncertainty and intrigue of real mathematics. Mathematicians do not sit at desks doing isolated problems. Instead, they discuss, debate, and argue—building theories and collecting data to support them, working cooperatively (and sometimes competitively) to refine and develop such theories further.

Mathematicians and scientists use information or data like snapshots to look at, describe, and better understand the world. They cope with the real-world "messiness" of the data they encounter, which often do not lead to a single, clear answer.

Because statistics is an application of real mathematics skills, it provides the opportunity to model real mathematical behaviors. As students engage in the study of statistics, they, like scientists and statisticians, participate in:

▼ cooperative learning

▼ theory building

▼ discussing and defining terms and procedures

▼ working with messy data

▼ dealing with uncertainty

We want elementary school students to have the opportunity to engage in such real mathematical behavior, discussing, describing, challenging each other, and building theories about real-world phenomena based on their work.

Data analysis in the mathematics curriculum

Exploring data involves students directly in many aspects of mathematics. Data are collected through counting and measuring; they are sorted and classified; they are represented through graphs, pictures, tables, and charts. In summarizing and comparing data, students calculate, estimate, and choose appropriate units. In the primary grades, work with data is closely tied to the number relationships and measuring processes that students are learning. In the upper elementary grades, students encounter some of the approaches used in statistics for describing data and making inferences. Throughout the data analysis process, students make decisions about how to count and measure, what degree of accuracy is appropriate, and how much information is enough; they continually make connections between the numbers and what those numbers represent.

Instead of doing mathematics as an isolated set of skills unrelated to the world of reality, students can understand statistics as the vibrant study of the world in which they live, where numbers can tell them many different stories about aspects of their own lives. The computation they do is for a purpose, and the analysis they do helps them to understand how mathematics can function as a significant tool in describing, comparing, predicting, and making decisions. ■

TEACHING DATA ANALYSIS

The nature of data analysis

In data analysis, students use numbers to describe, compare, predict, and make decisions. When they analyze data, they search for patterns and attempt to understand what those patterns tell them about the phenomena the data represent.

A data analysis investigation generally includes recognizable phases:

▼ considering the problem

▼ collecting and recording data

▼ representing the data

▼ describing and interpreting the data

▼ developing hypotheses and theories based on the data

These phases often occur in a cycle: the development of a theory based on the data often leads to a new question, which may begin the data analysis cycle all over again.

Elementary students can collect, represent, and interpret real data. Although their work differs in many ways from that of adult statisticians, their processes are very similar. Elementary school students can both analyze data and use those data to describe and make decisions about real situations.

Because real data are the basis for investigations in data analysis, there are no predetermined "answers." For example, if your class collects data on the ages of the students' siblings, the students understand that their job is more than simply coming up with an answer that you knew all along. Not only do you *not* know the answer in advance, but, without seeing the data, you may not even know what the most interesting questions are going to be!

While this situation encourages students to do their own mathematical thinking, it can also feel risky for you. Many teachers welcome a little uncertainty in their mathematics classes, when it prods their students to be more independent thinkers. To support you, the authors provide sample experiences from teachers who have used the activities described here so that you can be prepared for the kinds of issues that are likely to arise. You will soon build your own repertoire of experiences with data

analysis activities and will be able to anticipate likely questions, confusions, and opportunities.

The importance of discussion in mathematics

A central activity in data analysis is dialogue and discussion. While it is easy for you and your students to become engaged and enthusiastic in collecting data and making graphs, a significant amount of time should also be devoted to reflection about the meaning of the data.

Since students are not used to talking much during their mathematics work, it is important to support active decisionmaking by the students from the very beginning of the investigation. Students' participation in framing the initial question, choosing the methods of investigation, and deciding on ways to organize their data is essential. Once the data are collected and organized, the students must grapple with interpreting the results. If you have the outcome of a discussion or the "teaching points" you want to make too clearly in mind, you may guide students' observations too quickly into predetermined channels. When student ideas are ignored, misinterpreted, or rejected, they soon understand that their job is to second-guess the "answer" you had in mind.

On the other hand, if students find that *anything* they say is accepted in the same way, if every contribution is "a good idea" and no idea is ever challenged, they can lose motivation to participate. Ask students to reflect on, clarify, and extend their ideas and to listen to and ask questions of each other. Discussions in mathematics should encourage students to interpret numbers, make conjectures, develop theories, consider opposing views, and support their ideas with reasons.

Sensitive issues in data analysis

Students of all ages are interested in data about themselves and the issues they care about. Topics that matter enough to students to make them compelling topics for study often have very personal aspects. Investigations about families, heights, or students' chores, for example, can all bring up sensitive issues. After trying many topics in many classrooms, we have concluded that the potential sensitivity of a topic is not a reason to avoid it; on the contrary, these are the very topics that most engage student interest. All teachers deal with difficult or sensitive issues in their classroom, and the skills demanded of a teacher in handling issues that arise during data analysis activities are no different. Keep in mind that students may

sometimes want their data to be anonymous. Focusing on the patterns and shape of the class data, rather than on individual pieces of data, is particularly helpful, especially for upper elementary students.

Small-group work

Many of the investigations involve students working in teams. At first, keep small-group sessions short and focused. For students not used to working in small groups, assign specific tasks that encourage the participation of all the group members. For example, instead of, "Have a discussion in your group to decide what you want to ask the second graders about their bedtimes," you might say, "Come up with three possible questions you could ask the second graders."

Materials

Students need materials to represent their data during their investigations. These range from Unifix cubes to pencil and paper to computer software. What is most important is that students are able to construct multiple views of the data quickly and easily and that they do not become bogged down in drawing and coloring elaborate graphs (which are appropriate only at the very end of an investigation when students are ready to "publish" their findings).

Any material that can be moved easily and rearranged quickly offers possibilities for looking at data. For example, students might write or draw their data on *index*

cards (or any paper rectangles); then these can be arranged and rearranged. *Unifix cubes* (or other interconnecting cubes) are another good material for making representations throughout the grades. We have found that *stick-on notes* (such as Post-it notes), with each note representing one piece of data, are an excellent material for making rough drafts of graphs. They can be moved around easily and adhere to tables, desks, paper, or the chalkboard. *Pencil and unlined paper* should always be available for tallies, line plots, and other quick sketch graphs.

Calculators

Calculators should be available, if possible, throughout the activities. Their use is specifically suggested in some of the investigations. It is no secret to students that calculators are readily available in the world and that adults use them often. But many students do not know how to use a calculator accurately, do not check their results for reasonableness, and do not make sensible choices about when to use a calculator. Only through using calculators with appropriate guidance in the context of real problems can they gain these skills.

Computers

Computers are a key tool in data analysis in the world outside of school. Graphing software, for example, enables scientists and statisticians to display large sets of data quickly and to construct multiple views of the data easily. Some software for the elementary grades allows this flexibility as well. A finished graph made by the computer may, for some students, be an appropriate illustration for a final report of their findings. But keep in mind that students also make interesting and creative graphs by hand that would not be possible with the software available to them. Other computer software, including software for sorting and classifying and data base software, is particularly useful for some data analysis investigations. Where the use of a software tool would particularly enhance a data analysis investigation, recommendations for incorporating its use are made in the text and noted at the beginning of the session.

Home-school connections

Many opportunities arise in data analysis investigations for communicating with parents about the work going on in the classroom and for including them as participants in your data investigations. When you begin this unit, you may want to send a note home to parents explaining that students will be studying data analysis in their mathematics class and that, from time to time, parents can be of assistance in helping students collect data from home. Parents or other family members often provide an available comparison group. Studies of age, family size, height, and so forth can be extended to include parents. If students are studying their own families, they may be interested in collecting comparison data about their parents'

families. Including parents and other significant family members as participants in your data analysis investigations can stimulate their interest and enthusiasm for the work students are doing in school and, at the same time, help students see that the mathematics they do in school is connected to their life outside of school.

Interdisciplinary connections

Many teachers find ways to connect the data analysis experiences students have in mathematics to other areas of the curriculum. Data analysis is, after all, a tool for investigating phenomena of all kinds. The same approaches that students use in this unit can be called on for an investigation in science or social studies. Making these connections explicit and helping students transfer what they have learned here to new areas will give them an appreciation of the usefulness of mathematics throughout the curriculum. ■

MEASURING: FROM PACES TO FEET
UNIT OVERVIEW

Measuring: From Paces to Feet is a unit of study that introduces measuring as a way of collecting data. Suitable for students in grades 3 and 4, it provides a foundation for further work in statistics and data analysis, including the three upper-grade units in the *Used Numbers* series. In *Measuring: From Paces to Feet*, students:

▼ experience the iteration of a measurement unit, first with their own paces and later with more standardized units

▼ collect real data through measuring, using both informal and standard measurement systems

▼ represent measurement data in a variety of ways

▼ describe landmarks and features of the data

▼ formulate hypotheses and build theories about the reality represented by the data

How to use this unit

Like all the *Used Numbers* units, *Measuring: From Paces to Feet* is organized into investigations that may extend from one to four class sessions. To cover the entire unit requires approximately 17 class sessions of about 45 minutes each. Teachers who have used this unit have found that a schedule of 2–3 sessions per week works best to maintain continuity while allowing enough time for reflection and consolidation between sessions. The activities are sequenced so that students move gradually from more straightforward to more complex investigations. The investigations are grouped into three parts:

▼ **Part 1: Introduction to measurement**
How can we measure the room?
Robot paces
Paces come in different sizes

▼ **Part 2: Using standard measures**
Are our feet a foot long?
Using a smaller unit

▼ **Part 3: A project in data analysis**
Two options:
Classroom furniture: Do our chairs fit?
How close can you get to a pigeon?

The three parts work well as a single five- to six-week unit. Some teachers have substituted this unit for their textbook chapters on measurement or statistics. Others have used it late in the year as a way to consolidate students' mathematical learning, knowing that it brings together work in measurement, estimation, computation, graphing, and statistics in a problem-solving context. The parts can also be spaced over the entire school year. For example, some teachers use Part 1 in September to start off their work in mathematics. They return to Part 2 in January and use Part 3 in May when students have been together for most of the school year and are more able to work independently. Within each part, it is important that 2–3 sessions take place each week so that the experiences build on each other, allowing students gradually to acquire skills and understanding in data analysis.

In order to understand measurement, students need to experience it physically. This unit emphasizes using the body as a measuring tool; we believe students need to connect the counting of a repeated unit of measure with the repetitive physical movement of stepping and counting. As standard units we use inches and feet, which are not only based on human measurements, but are at present in more common use in the schools. For teachers who want to connect this unit with the metric system, a brief extension into making metric measurements can be added at the end of Part 2. Finding metric benchmarks on the body, taking metric measurements, and doing the final projects in metric measurements should follow naturally when the students realize that any imposed measurement system is a social convention, and that they can choose one of many systems to use.

Planning the investigations

In this book, you will find four types of information for each investigation:

Investigation overview. This section includes (1) a summary of the student activity, (2) materials you will need for the investigation and any special arrangements you may need to make, and (3) a list of the important mathematical ideas you will be emphasizing. Plan to look carefully at this overview a day or two before launching the investigation.

Session activities. For each session, you will find step-by-step suggestions that outline the students' explorations and the teacher's role. Although suggestions for questions and instructions are given, you will of course modify what you say to reflect your own style and the needs of your students. In all cases, the teacher's words are intended to be guidelines, *not* word-for-word scripts. Plan to read through this section before each session to get the general flow of the activities in your mind.

Dialogue Boxes. The Dialogue Boxes illustrate the special role of discussion in these investigations and convey the nature of typical student-teacher interactions. Examples are drawn from the actual experiences of classes that have used these investigations. They call attention to issues that are likely to arise, typical student confusions and difficulties, and ways in which you can guide and support students in their mathematical thinking. Plan to read the relevant Dialogue Boxes before each session to help prepare for interactions with your students.

Teacher Notes. These sections provide important information you will need in presenting this unit. Here you will find explanations of key aspects of measuring and of collecting and analyzing data, including ways to graph data and how and when to introduce special terms. The Teacher Notes are listed in the contents because many are useful as references throughout the unit, not just where they first appear. You might plan to read them all for background information before starting the unit, then review them as needed when they come up in particular investigations.

Goals for students

The "Important mathematical ideas" listed in the investigation overviews highlight the particular student goals for those sessions. The major goals for *Measuring: From Paces to Feet*, are as follows:

Part 1: Introduction to measurement

Moving through space and counting the movements. Students experience measurement through their own movements in space; by actively pacing and counting they learn how linear measurements are expressed in numbers.

Comparing units of measure. As they use different units of measure, students learn about the relationship between sizes of measuring units and the results of measuring. Students compare different units of measure as they use them, thus learning their relative sizes through use.

Estimating distances. Estimation of distance is an important process in internalizing a measurement system. A measurement system is internalized when students have stored some mental images or concepts that allow them to estimate fairly accurately.

Defining a measurement method. Through discussing the methods they will use to measure, students learn that defining measurement procedures is a critical part of data collection.

Writing directions involving distances. Writing and reading symbolic information about lengths and distances is an important measurement skill. This unit teaches those skills directly through an emphasis on giving and receiving both oral and written directions.

Recording and displaying the results of measurement. Students use a variety of data displays to show the results of their measurement investigations.

Part 2: Using standard measures

Experiencing a need to standardize. Students use standard measurements when they directly experience the variation that exists if standards are not developed.

Understanding that standard measures were invented to solve real data collection problems. Standardized measures are needed when measurement information is transmitted to another person. Students learn that data collected by measuring are not comparable unless the measures are agreed upon and have become a convention.

Estimating lengths. Students estimate lengths using feet and inches. They find benchmarks on their bodies that help them make reasonable estimates.

Measuring accurately, using feet and inches. When students are finding measurements to answer a question that involves them personally, the level of accuracy they will strive for is greatly increased.

Describing the shape of the data. Students learn to use simple statistical terms and concepts to describe the distribution of real data collected from their classroom measurement activities.

Analyzing data through landmarks and features of the data. Students begin to analyze data by interpreting the meaning of certain landmarks in the data: Which is the middle-sized foot? How can we describe the typical chair size in this classroom? By discussing and describing their data, students develop beginning skills in data analysis.

Using standard measures to compare data sets. The collection and comparison of two data sets—the length of student feet vs. the length of teacher feet—gives students experience in using, reporting, and recording data with standard measurement systems.

Part 3: A project in data analysis

Experiencing all the phases of a data analysis investigation in which measuring is used to collect data. Parallel to the phases of the writing process, a data analysis investigation includes "brainstorming" or discussion and definition of data collection methods; rough draft graphs of preliminary results; analyses leading to refinement of ideas, and final "publication" through reports of results. The final project in this unit gives students a chance to experience all phases of this process. ■

Measuring: From Paces to Feet

PART 1
Introduction to measurement

HOW CAN WE MEASURE THE ROOM?

INVESTIGATION OVERVIEW

What happens

Students participate in activities that link measurement to physical movement, counting their steps as they measure distances in the classroom. As the students collect data and compare their results, they begin to notice and analyze the numerical differences that are produced when they use units of different sizes.

The activities take three class sessions of about 45 minutes each.

What to plan ahead of time

▼ Play the game "Giant Steps" with the class. See the Teacher Note, *Playing "Giant Steps"* (page 16) for directions.

▼ For Session 1 you will need note cards or stick-on notes, such as Post-it notes,

on which students can write. If you use note cards or other pieces of paper, you may want to purchase a glue stick with a removable adhesive (such as Dennison's Tack-a-Note). This kind of glue lets you fasten pieces of paper temporarily to the chalkboard, converting them to stick-on notes. Keep these materials handy for sessions in which you are making line plots on the chalkboard or students are arranging and rearranging their data.

▼ Duplicate Student Sheet 1 (page 73) for each student (Session 1, homework).

▼ Duplicate Student Sheet 2 (page 74) for each pair of students (Session 3).

▼ Become familiar with making a line plot. See the Teacher Note, *Line plot: A quick way to show the shape of the data* (page 17).

☞ Save the data gathered in Session 1 for use in Session 2. See the Teacher Note, *What are data anyway?* (page 20) for a discussion of what we mean by "data."

Important mathematical ideas

Using a nonstandard unit to measure a distance. Students use their own giant steps, baby steps, and paces as units in measuring the length of the classroom. In making these measurements, they experience the iterative nature of measurement, counting the number of times an agreed-upon unit is used in moving from the beginning to the end of an object.

Estimating length. Students estimate length using paces. At first they estimate using their own paces or the paces of other members in the class. Students work at visualizing the unit repeated over a distance and share their methods with the class.

Comparing the effects of measurement using units of different size. A single distance can be described in different ways if we use different units of measure. Many third and fourth graders are confused by the fact that for the same distance, they get different results from their individual pacing. Repeated experiences help them understand that the different results come from using somewhat different units—that is, not all "paces" are identical. As they progress through these sessions, students begin to standardize their own units and to understand some reasons for using conventional measurement units. ■

SESSION 1 ACTIVITIES

Preparing for the session: Playing "Giant Steps"

Playing the game "Giant Steps" is an important prerequisite experience for the first sessions of this unit (see the Teacher Note, *Playing "Giant Steps,"* page 16). You may want to do this during class time, or you may prefer to play the game during a lunch or morning recess period.

Considering the problem: Estimating distance in giant steps

Remember when we played "Giant Steps"? Today we're going to estimate and then count distances in the room in giant steps.

Select a student to be the giant. The giant is to stand at the front of the classroom, then take two giant steps and freeze. Ask the other students to estimate the whole length of the classroom in those giant steps.

Make a picture in your head and try to imagine how many of [Ricardo's] giant steps it would take to get to the far wall.

Write the estimates on the board; then ask the giant to pace three more giant steps, and record any revision of the students' estimates. Next, as the giant paces the whole length of the room, have the students count out loud and record the answer.

You could each measure the length of the room in your own giant steps. Will all your answers be the same? What do you think?

Allow time for students to talk about whether they think there will be any variation in their results. Third and fourth graders have a wide range of theories about how and why measurement results might vary.

Collecting data: Measuring the length of the classroom

Establish student pairs that will pace the length of the classroom in giant steps. While one partner paces, the other counts. Students then switch roles. Ask students to record their results on the board. They may look like this:

13	14	12	13	14	13
11	12	14	$12\frac{1}{2}$		

Look at the numbers on the board. Did everyone get the same results? Is that surprising? Why or why not?

Recording and organizing the data: Line plots

Showing your students quick and effective ways of recording information gives them important tools they will need to investigate and analyze data. As you work together on these investigations, your quick sketching of students' results (using tallies, charts, line plots, and other kinds of informal data displays) will help them realize that data can be organized and displayed quickly in a variety of ways (see the Teacher Note, *Recording data*, page 17).

Because the idea of organizing data is probably new to your students, make a line plot on the board to show the results of their pacing off the room (see the Teacher Note, *Line plot: A quick way to show the shape of the data*, page 17). Draw a number line, label the points to include the smallest and largest numbers of giant steps, and show students how to make X's, check marks, or other symbols to record their data along the line.

```
                  X
           X      X      X
    X      X  X   X      X
  ┌──────────────────────────────┐
    11     12    13     14    15
```

Why do you get different results? Can you think of some reasons?

Allow time for students to discuss the variation in results (which will surprise some students more than others). There is much room here for theory-building. Many of your students will have theories that do not match yours. In one room, a student believed that people's steps automatically became bigger when they went slowly. Another believed paces varied because of foot size. These children were happy to talk about their ideas and to debate with their peers. The "odd" theories became the focal point for hypothesis-testing in the classroom, and

everyone felt good about the process. For all theories, ask students for their reasons and evidence, and support their thinking at this stage (see the Teacher Note, *Mathematical discussions: Challenging ideas*, page 18). Some of your students will have an easy time seeing that the size of a student's step makes a difference in numerical results; others won't. Inverse relationships—the smaller the pace, the bigger the number of paces—are hard to grasp, hold onto, and use.

Collecting data: Measuring in "baby steps"

Now you will measure the same distance, but you'll use baby steps. Do you think you'll get different results?

Allow a full discussion of students' predictions here, and when you think they're ready, ask someone to demonstrate baby steps.

Imagine, now, how many little steps like that it takes to get to the other wall. Try to imagine the baby steps in a straight path across the room. How many will it take?

Record students' predictions (this needn't be done elaborately), then pair up students to pace and count. If they write their results on index cards, they can enter the data quickly onto a line plot when everyone has finished pacing.

Baby steps produce much larger numbers than giant steps; your students will want to

talk about this. Why should the littlest steps give us the biggest numbers? Some third and fourth graders are confused by this; they will need to talk about it, try it, and work hard to understand that the bigger the step, the fewer the paces. It's important not to push the students who don't get it, but to keep asking them questions about their ideas.

☛ Save all the data for the next session; students will be comparing today's results with the results of their next activity.

Extensions

If you have time and your students' interest is high, you can repeat the activity with student pairs measuring the *width* of the classroom. Half the class might measure in giant steps, the other half in baby steps.

Student Sheet 1, *Giant steps and baby steps: Measuring at home*, encourages students to "measure" using giant steps or baby steps in their home environments. Depending on your homework policy, you may prefer to have students conduct a similar activity at school. ■

✎ TEACHER NOTE
Playing "Giant Steps"

This game (also called "Mother May I?") may be one your students know already. It usually involves 6–12 players. Optimal size is a group of about 10. You may want to divide your class and take turns playing—or if space allows, have two or three groups playing at once.

One player is the *caller*, who gives directions. The caller stands on an imaginary line facing the other players; they stand in a row about 15 to 20 feet away and move toward the caller as directed. The object of the game is to cross the line on which the caller stands. The first person over that line becomes the next caller. The caller gives directions to each player in turn, such as "Take 5 giant steps" or "Take 7 baby steps," typically giving different instructions to each player. After hearing the directions, the player to whom they were directed must ask, "May I?" The caller then gives permission to perform the action with the words, "You may." Gradually, players advance toward the caller. A player who forgets to ask "May I?" must go back to the starting line.

In some versions of the game, the player proposes a move ("May I take 6 baby steps?"), which the caller can either allow ("Yes, you may") or disallow with a substitution ("No, but you may take six banana twirls").

The repertoire of possible moves includes:

▼ giant steps (the longest steps possible for the individual)

▼ baby steps (heel to toe steps)

▼ banana twirls (putting hand on head, stepping forward, and turning 360° simultaneously)

▼ bunny hops (hopping with both feet at once)

▼ lamp post (lying on the ground with feet marking current position—player reaches as far forward as possible, and stands at that point)

▼ duck steps (squatting, holding onto ankles, walking forward, quacking and flapping arms simultaneously)

▼ anything else your students know (it will vary from one region to another)

Much of the game revolves around the caller imagining how many steps it will take to reach the finish line—and, of course, playing favorites about who will cross the line first to become the next caller. For your purposes, the point of the game is that students practice visualizing distances and use a variety of steps of different lengths.

As a variation, you might work specifically on visualizing measures of distance. Set yourself up as the caller and have two or three students stand in a row about 6 feet away. As you give directions (i.e., "Take 4 giant steps" or "Take 3 banana twirls"), ask the rest of the class to visualize whether the students will or will not reach you with that move. ■

Recording data

Graphs are traditionally the focus for instruction in statistics in the elementary grades, even though the process of doing statistics involves much more than simply making and reading graphs.

Most of us think of graphs as the endpoint of the data analysis process. Statisticians, however, use pictures and graphs during the process of analysis as tools for understanding the data. Representing data in a picture, table, or graph is an attempt to discover features of the data, to array the data in such a way that the shape of the data and the relationships among the data can be seen.

Our students must gain facility with creating representations that provide a first quick look at the data. Encourage students to create quick pictures, diagrams, tables, and graphs in order to get a feel for the data. Younger students use more concrete and pictorial representations for this work—interlocking cubes, real objects, their own pictures. In the upper grades, more work will be done with numerical representations.

The numbers, or data, collected by measuring and counting are the "stuff" of this measurement unit. Those numbers must represent real events and concrete experiences for students. For this reason, the early part of the unit stresses the physical act of pacing.

Comparing their results by analyzing simple line plots or tables of data becomes an important analytic tool for these students.

Unit graphs are most often used in the primary grades. These representations use one item to represent each piece of data. Because of this, each student can keep track of his or her own piece of data as it is classified, moved, re-sorted, and discussed. Line plots done "on the fly" to organize data while they are being discussed and analyzed do not need titles, labels, or vertical axes. These graphs are truly rough drafts and are quickly put on the board as data are collected. Such quickie graphs provide the focus for beginning data analysis (see the Teacher Note, *The shape of the data: Clumps, bumps, and holes*, page 22).

When you ask your students to talk about the shape of the data, the most important idea is that they should pay attention to the *overall shape* of the data. Where are data clumped? Is there more than one clump? Are there tall, tall peaks? Are there holes? Is it an even distribution? Questions like these will help the students talk about what they see and learn to describe the distributions of data that they gather by measuring. Gradually the traditional data analysis landmarks can be introduced as students' experiences prepare them for such numerical conventions as the mode, the median, the range, and the mean. ■

Line plot: A quick way to show the shape of the data

A line plot is a quick way to organize numerical data. It clearly shows the range of the data and how the data are distributed over that range. Line plots work especially well for numerical data with a small range.

This representation is often used as a working graph during data analysis. It is an initial organizing tool for beginning work with a data set, *not* a careful, formal picture used to present the data to someone else. Therefore, it need not include a title, labels, or a vertical axis. A line plot is simply a sketch showing the values of the data along a horizontal axis and X's to mark the frequency of those values in the data set. For example, if 15 students have just collected data on the number of paces it takes to walk the length of the classroom, a line plot showing these data might look like this:

```
                              X  X
                              X  X
                    X         X  X
                    X         X  X
          X               X  X  X  X
 _____
  9  10  11  12  13  14  15  16  17  18  19  20
```

From this display, we can quickly see that two-thirds of the students took either 18 or 19 paces. Although the range is from 11 to

19, the interval in which most data falls is from 16 to 19. The outlier, at 11, appears to be an unusual value, separated by a considerable gap from the rest of the data. (For further information, see the Teacher Note, *Statistical words to introduce as appropriate*, page 33.)

One advantage of a line plot is that we can record each piece of data directly as we collect it. To set up a line plot, start with an initial guess from students about what the range of the data is likely to be: What do you think the lowest number should be? How high should we go? Leave some room on each end of the line plot so that you can lengthen the line later if the range includes lower or higher values than you expected.

By quickly sketching data in line plots on the chalkboard, you provide a model of how such plots can provide a quick, clear picture of the shape of the data. ■

✎TEACHER NOTE
Mathematical discussions: Challenging ideas

One of the most important ideas in mathematics is that one's assertions should be subject to scrutiny and challenge. The history of mathematics is the history of debate and discussion, yet we do not see much discussion in most mathematics classes.

In fact, many students are convinced that there is always one right answer and one "best" procedure in mathematics class. This idea often leads them to be nervous if their answers seem to conflict. That feeling is reflected in the following discussion in a third grade classroom, which occurred when the students were working on a later investigation in this unit, *Paces come in different sizes*.

Students have measured their paces and recorded their results. Now they are trying to decide how to find their middle-sized pace, and the teacher is helping them decide on a method.

We still don't know what the middle-sized pace is. What do you suggest we do?

JENNIFER: Put them in order from largest to smallest.

MICHAEL: Compare them with the ones we decided were all in the middle.

Yes, but that might give us a problem since we don't know for sure that those really are in the middle. Could we do it two different ways and see if the results are the same?

KYLE: What if we do it two ways and get different middle people?

What do you think will happen?

ELENA: An argument!

Indeed, such a situation will likely produce a conflict with the two methods yielding two sets of results. But this kind of argument lies at the heart of mathematical discussion. Encouraging students to make assertions, to base their arguments on data, to state their reasons, and to ask others clarifying questions is a vital aspect of teaching mathematics.

Challenging students' ideas is a delicate matter, yet it can be a very effective way of probing to find out what your students are thinking and to help them clarify and extend their own ideas. Many teachers find that the best way of examining students' ideas is to ask questions that invite them to explain their reasons.

Say more about that.

Can you give me an example?

How do the data tell you that?

Another technique is to ask students to relate their ideas to other students' ideas.

Is this like Su-Mei's idea?

Are your reasons the same as Jeremy's?

A third way teachers sometimes probe students' ideas is to give counterexamples.

Some other third [fourth] graders say that it's not the one that's chosen the most, but the one in the middle. What would you tell them?

Do you think that would work if we measured something else?

You may have other techniques that work for you. Once ideas are flowing, you may find that the students themselves make many suggestions, ask each other probing questions, and help to formulate ideas. Until then, however, it is important to keep discussion alive. Researchers have found that simply waiting 3 seconds after asking a question gives students time to organize their thinking and to develop some of their ideas before answering. Three seconds seems like a very long time when you're used to much faster answers, but students need to feel that they have time to think and time to make suggestions. Hurrying them to an answer defeats the whole purpose of mathematical discussions. ■

SESSION 2 ACTIVITIES

Considering the problem: Pacing the classroom

Recently we measured the length of our classroom in giant steps and baby steps. The stretch of taking giant steps and the finickiness of taking baby steps can be uncomfortable, though. A more widely used measurement is the *pace*, which is closer to a regular step. How can we measure someone's *pace*? Let's try with a volunteer.

Ask one student to take 3 or 4 regular walking steps, then freeze. Ask the class how long they think the room is in paces of that size. After they estimate the distance, have the same student pace off the length of the room while the class counts to keep track.

Collecting and describing data: Comparing different steps

Working in the same pairs as in the previous session, the students estimate and count the number of paces it will take them to measure the length of the classroom. Record their data on the chalkboard. One technique that works well is simply to record the data in a list, and then model a quick, effective way to organize it. A line plot is a good representation for these data (see the Teacher Note, *Line plot: A quick way to show the shape of the data*, page 17).

Let's record our results in a line plot. We need to decide on the beginning and end of the number line we'll use. Any ideas?

What can we see from this line plot? What can you say about the data?

Help students express their ideas as they describe the distribution of the data (see the Teacher Note, *The shape of the data: Clumps, bumps, and holes*, page 22).

What do you see in the graph? Do you see any clusters of data? Did most of you get the same number of paces when you measured the length of the room? Is the range of data very wide? Are there any unusual values?

For an example of such a discussion, see the Dialogue Box, *Describing the shape of the data* (page 21).

In another line plot, put the results of the previous session on the board and ask students to compare those data with their new results.

What can we say about our paces, our giant steps, and our baby steps? How do they compare?

This is likely to produce a long discussion of the relationship between step size and number of steps. Students will argue with each other about this relationship and about reasons for the difference in results. They may have trouble articulating their ideas, and some will not be able to put their ideas into words. Students may assert that it takes more steps for bigger people; others will assert that it's fewer—again, the inverse relationship (the bigger the person the fewer the steps) may confuse some of your students. Some teachers who have worked with this unit believe that the fact that smaller numbers "win" here is unusual and important, so that students do not just look at large numbers without evaluating what they represent. (See the Dialogue Box, *Discovering children's beliefs about numbers*, page 23, for another example of a mathematical side trip away from data analysis into more general beliefs.)

Questions like the following can produce fruitful discussion:

Which are the biggest steps? Did you take more baby steps or more giant steps? Why? If I take 6 giant steps to walk along here, will I take about 30, or about 10, or more like 3 baby steps to cover the same distance?

Make sure that students give reasons for their statements. Just as in the previous session, some students will not grasp all of the connections between size of step and number of steps taken. At this point, be satisfied that you are providing experiences that will lay the foundation for understanding. ■

✎ TEACHER NOTE
What are data, anyway?

I'm 48 inches tall.

This bottle holds 2 liters of soda pop.

She is wearing sneakers.

These shoes weigh 150 grams.

Each of these statements contains descriptive information or *data* about some person or thing. *Data* is a plural noun; one *datum* is a single fact. Data are the facts, or the information, that differentiate and describe people, objects, or other entities (e.g., countries). Data may be expressed as numbers (e.g., he is 48 inches tall; she has 4 people in her family) or attributes (her favorite flavor is chocolate; his hair is curly).

Data are collected through surveys, observation, measurement, counting, and experiments. If we study rainfall, we might collect rain and measure the amount that falls each day. If we study hair color, we might collect and record the color of each person's hair.

Collecting data involves detailed judgments about how to count, measure, or describe. Should we record rainfall data for each day or for each rainstorm? Should we round off to the nearest inch? Should we count just one color for a person's hair? Should we record "yellow" or "dirty blond" or "gold"?

Should "brown" be a single category, or should it be divided into several shades?

Once data are collected, recorded, counted, and analyzed, we can use them as the basis for making decisions. In one school, for example, a study of accidents on a particular piece of playground equipment showed that most of the accidents involved children who were in first, second, or third grade. Those who studied the data realized that the younger students' hands were too small to grasp the bars firmly enough. A decision to keep primary grade children off this equipment was made because the *data*, or the *facts*, led to that conclusion.

When students collect data, they are collecting facts. When they interpret these data, they are developing theories or generalizations. The data provide the basis for their theories. ■

66 99 DIALOGUE BOX
Describing the shape of the data

The students have just counted the number of paces it takes each of them to walk the length of the classroom. They have recorded their data on a line plot and are beginning to talk about what they can see.

```
            X
            X   X
X   X   X   X   X
X   X   X   X   X           X               X
14  15  16  17  18  19  20  21  22  23  24
```

So what can you say about these pace data? Let's hear a few of your ideas.

SEAN: Well, there are a lot at 16.

SHANTA: There was only one at 20 and one at 23.

VALERIE: There are two each at 14 and 15.

What else do you notice?

ARACELI: Fourteen is the lowest.

So no one took fewer than 14 paces?

BENJAMIN: Yeah. And 23 was the highest.

So the *range* was from 14 to 23. What else?

SUSAN: There's nothing at 19, 21, or 22.

Susan's noticing that there are a lot of holes in this part of the data. Can anyone say any more about that?

MICHAEL: Well, there's nothing at 12 or 13 either.

Yes, 14 is the lowest count and there's nothing below it. But this situation, that Susan noticed up here, is a little different. What can you say about that?

SU-MEI: Mostly, the paces go from 14 to 18, but sometimes you get something higher.

Can anyone add to that?

SEAN: You must have really small paces if it takes you 23.

In fact, mathematicians have a name for a piece of data that is far away from all the rest. They call it an *outlier*. An outlier is an unusual piece of data—sometimes it might actually be an error, but sometimes it's just an unusual piece of data. It's usually interesting to try to find out more about an outlier. Who had the outlier in this case?

BOBBY: I did. And I counted twice, and Michael checked me, too, so I know it was 23 paces.

JENNIFER: Maybe he's got smaller feet.

Any other theories about Bobby's pace?

[Later] . . .

So if someone asked you, "What's the typical number of paces to cross our classroom?"— what would you say?

TAMARA: Well, I'd say 16.

[Addressing the class as a whole, not just the student who answered] **Would 16 be a reasonable description of how many paces long our room is?**

CHRIS: I think so, because most of us took 16 paces.

Any other ways to say this? Or any different ideas?

PEGGY: Well, I wouldn't say just 16.

Why not?

PEGGY: Well, there's really not that much difference between 16, 17, and 18. They're all really close together. I'd say 14 to 18, cause the 20 and 23 aren't what you'd usually get.

So Peggy is saying she'd use an *interval* to describe the pace-length of our room, from 14 to 18, and Chris said he'd say the length was about 16. What do other people think about that?

☛ In this discussion, the class has moved gradually from describing individual features of the data to looking at the shape of the data as a whole. The teacher introduced the ideas of *interval*, *range*, and *outlier* because they came up in the discussion and were appropriate in describing these data (see the Teacher Note: *Statistical words to introduce as appropriate*, page 33). Throughout the conversation, the teacher tries to have students give reasons for their ideas and pushes them to think further by asking for additions or alternatives to ideas students have raised. ■

The shape of the data: Clumps, bumps, and holes

Describing and interpreting data is a skill that must be acquired. Too often, students simply read numbers or other information from a graph or table without any interpretation or understanding. It is easy for students to notice only isolated bits of information (e.g., "Vanilla got the most votes," "Five people were 50 inches tall") without developing any overall sense of what the graph shows. Looking at individual numbers in a data set without looking for patterns and trends is something like decoding the individual words in a sentence without comprehending the meaning of the sentence.

To help students pay attention to the shape of the data—the patterns and special features of the data—we have found it useful to use such words as *clumps, clusters, bumps, gaps, holes, spread out, bunched together,* and so forth. Encourage students to use this casual language about shape to describe where most of the data are, where there are no data, and where there are isolated pieces of data.

A discussion of the shape of the data often breaks down into two stages. First, we decide what are the special features of the shape:

Where are the clumps or clusters, the gaps, the outliers? Are the data spread out, or are lots of the data clustered around a few values? Second, we decide how we can interpret the shape of these data: Do we have theories or experience that might account for how the data are distributed?

As an example, consider the following sketch graph of the weights (in pounds) of 23 lions in U.S. zoos.

25–49	✓	✓	
50–74			
75–99			
100–124	✓	✓	
125–149			
150–174			
175–199			
200–224	✓		
225–249	✓		
250–274			
275–299	✓	✓	✓
300–324	✓	✓	✓
325–349	✓	✓	
350–374	✓		
375–399	✓		
400–424	✓	✓	✓
425–449	✓		
450–474	✓	✓	✓

(Source: Zoos in Atlanta, Cleveland, Little Rock, Memphis, Miami, the Bronx, Philadelphia, Rochester, San Antonio, and Washington, DC. Data collected in 1987.)

In the first stage of discussion, students observed the following special features:

▼ There is a clump of lions between 400 and 475 pounds (about a third of the lions).

▼ There is another cluster centering around 300 pounds (another third).

▼ There are two pairs of much lighter lions, separated by a gap from the rest of the data.

In the second stage of discussion, students considered what might account for the shape of these data. They immediately theorized that the four lightest lions must be cubs. They were, in fact, one litter of 4-month-old cubs in the Miami Zoo. The other two clusters turned out to reflect the difference between the weights of adult male and female lions.

Throughout this unit, we strive to steer students away from merely reading or calculating numbers drawn from their data (e.g., the range was 23 to 48, the median was 90, the biggest height was 52 inches). These numbers are useful only when they are seen in the context of the overall shape and patterns of the data set and when they lead to questioning and theory-building. By focusing instead on the broader picture—the shape of the data—we discover what those data have to tell us about the world. ■

DIALOGUE BOX
Discovering children's beliefs about numbers

Children have many ideas about numbers that are not always apparent in the classroom. One of the benefits of mathematical discussions is that those ideas can surface and be talked about.

Here, for instance, is a discussion that surfaced in a third grade classroom while students were analyzing a data display produced in the investigation *Using a smaller unit*. The display showed the lengths of their feet in inches. They were looking for the middle-sized foot.

```
                X     X     X
                X     X     X  X  X
        X   X   X     X  X  X  X
      ────────────────────────────────
       6  6½  7  7½  8  8½  9  9½ 10  10½ 11
```

VALERIE: I think 8 is in the middle because 9-1/2 and 10-1/2 aren't numbers, they're halves. Then if you match 6 and 10, and 7 and 9, 8 is in the middle.

TAMARA: I think you should count 9-1/2 and 10-1/2 too, because they're numbers.

RICARDO: I think so too.

VALERIE: I still think that 1/2 numbers aren't regular numbers.

ELENA: But we have to count those numbers because those numbers have *people*. We don't need to count the other halves because nobody has those numbers.

VALERIE: I get it. I think we should count them too, but only if they have people.

The discussion clearly had two threads—the "reality" of the fractional numbers, and the search for the middle-sized foot. The students resolved it by granting reality to the halves when they represented real values (i.e., if they "had people").

The teacher did not take an active role in this discussion, preferring that the students talk among themselves about whether the numbers were real or not. She was surprised by their idea that halves weren't numbers, and decided to follow up in a different context at a later date.

Gaps between children's intuitive, informal understanding of numbers and their school knowledge do not always arise unless there is some reason to talk in a fairly open-ended way about numbers used in a real context. One of the important benefits of mathematical discussions is the chance to hear students expressing their intuitive beliefs about numbers. Informal diagnosis of children's understanding is often based on such conversations. ■

SESSION 3 ACTIVITIES

Collecting and recording data: Estimates and actual distances

Ask one student to stand in a fairly open part of the classroom. Select a target that is a moderate distance away *in a straight line*. Have the student take three or four *paces* to help the others visualize the length of a pace.

You may want to dramatize the visualization process by "thinking through" your own way of making an estimate:

Let's see—I can see how long Shanta's pace is, so I'll try to imagine: 2 . . . 3 . . . 4 . . . 5 . . . 6. About 6 paces to the desk, I think. Let's try it! . . . Now, how many paces is it from Shanta to the globe?

Students estimate, the pacer paces the distance, and everyone counts. Repeat this two or three times, selecting different objects. You may want to use more than one student as a pacer.

Next break the class into two-person teams that will work in different parts of the room. Give each team a copy of Student Sheet 2, *Pacing in pairs*. On each team, one student is the *caller* and the other is the *pacer*. Each team marks a starting place, and the caller selects an object or location in the classroom that can be reached on a straight line. The pacer then demonstrates a "typical" pace, and both students estimate the distance in those paces. As the pacer walks to the target, both students count to keep track; they record the results on Student Sheet 2.

Extension: Estimating other distances

The student teams may develop some good strategies for estimating distances in paces. To practice these strategies, follow up with a whole-class activity. Select various points in the classroom and ask everyone to estimate the number of a specific student's paces between the points. Write down all estimates, then check by pacing to see how close the class estimates are. Visual estimation is an important component of measurement, and practice does make a difference! ∎

ROBOT PACES

INVESTIGATION OVERVIEW

What happens

Students give directions to move from one point to another, taking turns being the direction-giver or the robot who follows directions. At first these directions involve stating a number of paces to move forward. Gradually the directions become more complex and include right and left turns. Partners compare the number of paces they take from one spot to another, learning to estimate the number of their partner's paces it takes to go from A to B. Differences in pace size and the effects of those differences on numerical results are experienced and discussed. Learning to count off units (in this case, paces) along an unmarked distance provides students the opportunity to measure with familiar units.

The activities take three class sessions of about 45 minutes each.

What to plan ahead of time

▼ Provide paper plates as targets, one for each pair of students. Write a number or letter on each plate to differentiate them.

▼ Duplicate Student Sheet 3 (page 75), Student Sheet 4 (page 76), and Student Sheet 5 (page 77) for each pair of students (Sessions 2 and 3).

▼ Have calculators available (Session 3).

Important mathematical ideas

Estimating distance to a point in space. Students will be giving directions to each other that involve careful estimation of distance, given a particular unit. Some will need help in finding ways to make effective estimates; they may need more experience than these sessions alone provide. Encourage stu-

dents to practice their estimation skills at home and on the playground as well.

Comparing lengths of routes. Students compare the lengths of routes and learn that the segments of a distance, when added, yield the whole distance traveled.

Giving directions to another person. First orally, and then in writing, students give directions that involve nonstandard measurement of distance. The progression from oral to written directions is important to students' understanding of written information about measurement. Help them to read each other's directions by making "mental maps" of the routes being described. ■

SESSION 1 ACTIVITIES

Considering the problem: How can we give good directions?

If someone asks you for directions to another place, it's important to give them good directions. Today you will pretend to be robots and practice giving directions by telling each other how far to move.

Demonstrate the task in front of the class. Ask for a volunteer robot, who must do exactly what you say. Put a paper plate some distance away from the robot; this is your target. Give directions that will move the robot to the target paper plate. Use only "forward" or "backward" commands at this time; you will be making turns a little later. Say, for example:

Robot, go 5 paces forward.

Assess the effect of this movement with the class.

Does the robot need to be given new directions? Did my estimate as the direction-giver work for this particular robot?

Students work in pairs, taking turns being the robot. Give each team a paper plate identified by a number or letter. The direction-giver positions the plate, tells the robot how many paces to take toward the target, and assesses the success of his or her directions. Then students swap roles. They do

this twice, then return to their seats.

Was this difficult? Were your estimates of distance fairly accurate?

Encourage students to talk about their experiences, calling attention to the issue of estimating distance in paces.

Considering the problem: Making turns

It's usually harder to give directions in real life, because you can't always go in a straight line to get somewhere. The person who's asking for directions will probably have to turn at least once to reach the goal. We'll practice making turns and measuring distances that aren't in a straight line. First, I need another volunteer robot.

Give directions to the robot that involve making turns.

Robot, turn left. . . . Robot, go 4 paces forward. . . . Robot, turn right.

Help students establish a working definition of a turn. Most classes decide that a turn is a 90° turn, or a square corner. Point out a target in the classroom and give directions to the robot as a demonstration. The robot is to move as directed after each command.

Students again pair up, one being the direction-giver and the other the robot. As before, they use the paper plates to mark target points, but this time the directions will require the robot to make turns. Remind stu-

dents to give just one direction at a time.

Considering the problem: Preparing written directions

After students have had the chance to both give and respond to oral directions, call them back into the whole group for some discussion before starting the next phase of this activity.

Let's hear from the direction-givers first, and then the robots. What was hard about this task? What was easy?

The next time we give directions to robots, we will still be doing pacing and turning, but you'll be writing down your directions first, so you can keep a record of them.

Demonstrate this with a volunteer robot. Write directions on the board that will get the robot to some unnamed target. Use just two forward commands and one turn; for instance: *Forward 9 paces. Turn right. Forward 3 paces.*

Ask students to imagine the robot starting and pacing, and to tell where they think the robot will end up. Encourage them to visualize a robot's pace and to place that pace down over and over. This is very hard mental work and requires much concentration. When most of the students have made their estimates of the finishing point, ask the robot to follow the directions.

Did the robot end up where you expected?

Were you close? How did you make your estimate? How far did the robot travel in all? How many paces did the robot take altogether?

One important aspect of measuring is the ability to combine many small measurements into a total. Adding the smaller distances to find the full length of the robot's trip will help to lay the foundation for understanding relationships between small distances and longer ones.

Extension: Using the computer and the Logo language

If you and your students have access to Logo, using the Logo language on the computer is a logical extension and reinforcement of these activities. Giving and responding to directions about turns and distances is similar to moving the Logo turtle around the screen. You can organize the task so that one student points to a place on the screen and the other moves or programs the turtle to get to that spot. You can save the pictures or the programs and have students share and compare their solutions.

Extension: Practicing at home

Encourage students to pace off distances at home to practice their estimation and measurement skills.

What's the length of your bed in paces? What's your path to the kitchen sink from your bed? Suppose the path from your bedroom to the

kitchen is forward 3 paces, turn right, forward 16 paces, turn left; then how would you tell someone how to get from the kitchen to your bedroom?

You and the students might create a worksheet for recording the distances they have decided to pace off at home. ∎

Preparing for the next session: Writing directions with turns

Remember when I wrote directions on the board, telling a robot how to move? Today you'll be doing that in your teams. When you write, you will be writing down the same thing you would say to the robot.

Choose a volunteer robot again. Place a paper plate on the floor fairly near you, making sure that your demonstration robot can get to it with only one turn. Ask the whole class to visualize how the robot could get to the target. Write the directions on the board again: *Forward 3 paces. Turn left. Forward 2 paces.*

Ask students if they think these directions will get the robot to the paper plate. Then have the robot follow the directions to find out whether they work. Repeat the process with the whole class until everyone is clear about the task (see the Teacher Note: *Connecting oral and written directions*, page 28).

☞ Some third and fourth graders, as you well know, aren't sure about which direction is left and which is right. Some may need a good deal of experience making turns before they can function smoothly on this task.

Have students pair up. Give each pair a copy of Student Sheet 3, *Pacing and turning*, on which students will write robot directions for each other. Each team works cooperatively to position the paper plate targets, and to write the directions for the robot. The robot then paces the distance as directed. At this time, the directions should involve no more than one turn. When you think the class has had enough practice, call them back together for a discussion.

Was it hard to write down the directions? I suspect for some of you it was harder than saying them. What are some good strategies for deciding what to write down?

It's important that students talk about their strategies. Let them share their methods with their classmates.

Further preparation: Making many turns

Now we're going to make up some more complicated directions. Let's pick a starting point in the classroom and a target. Michael, be our robot and start from here [the corner of my desk]. We're going to write directions to get the robot to [the fish tank], and we're going to make him turn more than twice along the way. OK? Araceli, write our directions on the board as we decide what they should be. What should we tell the robot first? Forward how many paces? And turn which way? And now?

Lead the students to dictate directions that they think will get the robot to the target. If they seem ready for it, have them dictate all the directions first, and then ask the robot to follow those directions and see if they lead to the target. If, on the other hand, your students seem to need more experience, have

them dictate one direction at a time, write it on the board, and ask the robot to follow just that part of the directions.

Give each pair of students a copy of Student Sheet 4, *Making many turns.*

Working in pairs, *write* a set of directions to get your robot from the *same* place our robot started to the same target where our robot ended up. Try to find some different routes to get from here to there. The only rule is that you have to make the robot turn more than twice.

Students are to write directions that involve more than one turn. Some may have trouble doing this; it is a complicated task. ∎

✎ *TEACHER NOTE*
Connecting oral and written directions

When students give oral directions and commands to a "robot," they can see the effect of their words immediately. Creating a series of written directions, however, involves taking on another person's orientation in space. Telling the robot whether to turn right or left when the robot is facing in a different direction is very difficult.

Sometimes students need time to realize that the directions they write down are just the same as those they would have said out loud. It may help them to think through the effects of one move at a time, jotting down the directions as they think them. Sometimes students may need to write out and then check their directions.

Orientation in space is a complicated issue for students of this age. Some are better able than others to visualize the movement of someone else in space. Many students will need more experience before they can visualize turning left and right from another's point of view. These variations in ability are typical for third and fourth graders. Working carefully through this investigation and listening to other students describe their visualization methods will help students who are more hesitant. ∎

SESSION 3 ACTIVITIES

Collecting data: Planning and comparing robot routes

Today we're going to write directions for lots of robot routes. When we're finished we'll compare those routes.

Give a copy of Student Sheet 5, *Mapping and measuring*, to each pair of students. They will work together to generate three routes from designated starting points to designated targets. Before they begin, help them decide, as a class, on the three starting points and three ending points. Write these on the board as they are confirmed, and be sure each pair records the starting and ending points on the student sheet before devising their routes.

Students then add up the total number of paces in each route. Let them use calculators to check and compare the distances of their routes.

Describing the data: Finding the shortest route

We've found a lot of routes! Let's look first at routes between [the office] and [the library]. Choose your team's shortest route, and then we'll compare to see whose is the shortest of all. One of you read your route aloud.

As one student reads the pair's shortest route, record it in a large grid on the board

TEAM	ROUTE							TOTAL PACES
Elena and Kelly	Forward 2	Right	Forward 7	Left	Forward 9	Right	Forward 5	23
Barbara and Kim	Forward 4	Right	Forward 2	Left	Forward 4	Right	Forward 10	20
Shanta and Jeremy	Forward 6	Right	Forward 3	Left	Forward 6	Right	Forward 10	25

or on the overhead projector so that the whole class can see it, as shown above. Record only the shortest route for each pair.

Whose route is longest? Whose is the shortest? Is there something special about the shortest route of all?

Follow the same procedure to find the longest route any pair has developed. Compare and discuss these routes.

We've spent time finding the very shortest route and the very longest route you wrote down. Can you find an even longer one? Yes, Ray, come up and show us. Carl, you come too. . . . Can anyone think of an even longer one? Talk with your partner and together write down the very longest route from [the desk] to [the globe] that you can think of.

You'll find that the students can generate even longer routes once they start to have fun with the task. Just as you can always find a larger number by adding one more, you can always find a longer route by adding some turns or some backward steps.

Students' strategies for getting the longest distance involve overshooting the target and turning a lot, and will produce a good laugh for the whole class. This part of the session should result in some shared enjoyment, but more important, it will give the students a sense that they know how to give directions, with turns, using measurements to describe distance. This activity is a good place to use calculators; have one or two students pace a route while the others add up the paces they've used. ■

PACES COME IN DIFFERENT SIZES

INVESTIGATION OVERVIEW

What happens

Students pace routes to distant landmarks in the school and compare their results. Differences in results lead to an attempt at standardization of measure by finding the middle-sized pace of the students in the classroom, and using that as a standard pace.

The activities take two class sessions of about 45 minutes each.

What to plan ahead of time

▼ Duplicate Student Sheet 6 (page 78) for each pair of students (Session 1).

▼ Have calculators available (Session 1).

▼ Provide adding machine tape and scissors (Session 2). Adding machine

tape comes in thin rolls of different widths, available in stationery stores, office supply stores, and many drug stores and five and dimes. A roll typically costs less than a dollar, and three will probably be enough for all the activities in this unit. A width of about one inch works well.

Important mathematical ideas

Finding a standard of measure. The "middle-sized pace" is proposed to students as a standard that will reduce the variation in their measurement of distances. The focus of these sessions is on finding the advantages of standardizing their paces and achieving more uniform results.

Defining and refining measurement methods. There are different ways to measure a

pace, and students need to agree on a single method. In this investigation, students spend a good deal of time arguing about and defining their preferred methods of measurement. Support them by asking for demonstrations of their proposed methods, by recording on the board their final decisions about a method of measuring, and by calling their attention to questions that may arise during the data collection because of the method they have chosen.

Displaying data and finding the middle. After students compare their paces by direct measure, they need to find ways of displaying and organizing their data so they can determine the middle-sized pace. In this investigation, students consider methods for finding the middle of a data set. Help the students talk about these methods and refine their ideas about what is the "middle" of the data. ■

SESSION 1 ACTIVITIES

Considering the problem: Pacing to distant targets

We've been measuring distances in our class-room by pacing them. Today you'll be pacing much longer distances within the school build-ing. We'll all agree on three targets to pace to, but they can be anywhere in the school. How will this be different from pacing inside the classroom?

Have students pair up; give each pair a copy of Student Sheet 6, *Pacing to distant targets*. As the class chooses three targets in the school, write their choices on the board. Students then write each target in a box on Student Sheet 6.

In each pair, one of you will be the pacer and one the recorder. As you make your way to the target, you will record both paces and turns. Once you get to the target, return to the class-room with your jobs swapped—the one who paced will read the directions to the pacer, and the one who wrote will follow those directions and do the pacing. Your right and left turns will be different, but see whether your paces work.

Recording and describing data: How many paces did we take?

What happened as you paced these longer dis-tances? Did you run into any problems? Did other pairs share those difficulties?

Ask students questions that encourage them to reflect on their experiences. In some cases, they will have found that their numbers of paces did not match over long distances. Students use a variety of methods to solve that problem, including writing down each person's paces and trying to figure out why differences occurred.

In order to compare results within the whole class, ask students to count their total paces to each of the locations. Be sure that calculators are readily available.

What is the closest target location? The far-thest? The middle location? Did the number of paces surprise you?

One of the important aspects of statistics is the study of variation, or the differences among related data. For one of the target lo-cations, make a line plot and record the number of paces that each pair of students took to get to that location.

What do you notice? How can you describe these data? Are the distances pretty much the same? Or are they spread out? Are there clumps? Outliers? What might explain the things we notice about the data?

Help students talk about the data and the variation (see the Teacher Note, *Statistical words to introduce as appropriate*, page 33).

As students look at the variation in the total number of paces they took to get to these lo-cations, they will have many theories about why their results are different. Some of them may want to make a standard pace and use that; others won't be bothered by the varia-tion in results.

Describing the data: Comparing routes

Your students may be interested in compar-ing their actual routes. The routes them-selves can be recorded (as in the previous sessions) and compared on a large grid. One third grade teacher used the following format in her classroom. Her students had used the Logo language in their computer classes, and they suggested using the Logo abbreviations for Forward, Right, and Left:

Ray/Kim	FD 19	RT	FD 52	RT	FD 19	RT	FD 28
Susan/Chris	FD 24	RT	FD 63	RT	FD 15	RT	FD 30
Bobby/Sean	FD 29	RT	FD 80	RT	FD 46	RT	FD 45

How are your routes all the same? How are they different? Do you have some ideas about why the results might be different? Suppose we wanted to give directions to a school visi-tor, explaining how to get from the front door of the school to our classroom. Ray and Kim might tell our visitor to take 125 paces, while Susan and Chris might say to take 138 paces. How could we make these directions more similar, so that our visitor would be sure to find our classroom?

Chances are your students will suggest some rules for pacing; if they don't think of using a standard pace, you can suggest it. If students propose using standard measures such as inches or feet, you may want to respond, "Yes—inches or feet would be a good way. But let's focus on paces for today, and look at other measurements a little later." Students may have better ideas than we do, though, so be sure not to shut off discussion. ∎

✎ TEACHER NOTE
Statistical words to introduce as appropriate

Range and *outlier* are two statistical ideas that come up naturally while discussing data with students.

The range of the data is simply the interval from the lowest value to the highest value in the data set. The range of the data in the line plot below, showing how many paces it took each of 15 students to walk the length of the classroom, is from 11 to 19:

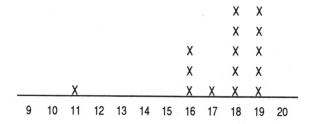

An outlier is an individual piece of data that has an unusual value, much lower or much higher than most of the data. That is, it "lies outside" the overall shape and pattern of the data. There is no one definition of how far away from the rest of the data a value must be to rate mention as an outlier. Although statisticians have rules of thumb for finding outliers, these are always subject to judgment about a particular data set. As you view the shape of the data, you and your students must judge whether there are values that really don't seem to fit with the rest of the data. For example, in the pace data, the measure of 11 paces for crossing the room seems to be an outlier.

Both *range* and *outliers* are ideas that will come up naturally as students work with different data sets in this unit. They can be introduced as soon as they arise in the students' descriptions of their data. Students easily learn the correct terms for these ideas and are particularly interested in outliers. Outliers should be examined closely. Sometimes they turn out to be mistakes—someone counted, measured, or recorded incorrectly—but other times they are simply unusual values. Students are usually very interested in building theories about these odd values: What might account for them?

Because of the nature of the data students collect in this unit on measuring, you are not very likely to find significant outliers in most of the data sets. You will, however, need to be alert to the possibility of outliers in data collected over greater distances, since small differences in measurement units become large differences when the distance itself is greater. Outliers may also appear in data collected at home. Extremely tall or extremely young brothers and sisters can skew the foot-size data, and students will enjoy talking about why someone's foot size might be so small or so very large. Third and fourth graders enjoy contemplating extremes. ∎

SESSION 2 ACTIVITIES

Considering the problem: Finding a standard pace

When we talked about giving directions to help a visitor find our classroom, a number of you wanted to find one pace for everyone to use when they walked, so that our directions would always come out the same. Today we will look at everyone's pace and try to find the middle-sized pace to use as a standard. That way you'll all be able to give similar directions. How could we go about finding the middle-sized pace?

Listen to all their ideas about solving this problem (see the Dialogue Box, *Finding the middle-sized pace*, page 35). List ideas on the board as they come up so that students can develop and modify each others' plans. This should be considered an introductory discussion to get them thinking about the problem; they need not settle on a plan at this time.

☛ Some of your students will suggest that you standardize these measurements by using inches or feet. They will "get it"! Others, though, won't even think about standard units of measurement until later in this unit. For those students, it's important to hold off on the standard units of measure for a while. If someone suggests inches or feet, you might respond, "That's a good idea, Jeremy, but let's wait. We'll use them later."

Collecting data: Measuring paces

How could we find the length of everyone's pace? Let's start out by finding how long my pace is. How could we use this paper tape?

Solicit ideas for measuring your pace directly. Take two or three paces and freeze Have two student volunteers mark your pace on the tape and use scissors to cut it to size, following directions from the class. There is lots of opportunity for discussion here, and students need to agree on a single method before the volunteers cut the tape. Will they measure toe to toe or heel to heel? (A surprising number want to measure toe to heel!) Be sure that they give reasons for choosing a particular method. You may need to dramatize the differences between suggested methods by having the volunteers cut many different tapes for your pace, following the different methods, and then compare them.

Once the class has settled on a method, establish working groups of two or three and give each group a pair of scissors, a pencil, and a length of adding machine tape. Helping one another, students in a group cut the adding machine tape to the length of each individual's pace. Writing names on the pace-tapes will help later when students compare sizes.

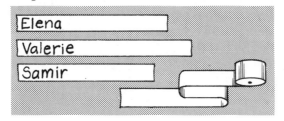

Organizing and describing data: Looking at everyone's pace

As the groups finish, tape their pace-tapes randomly to the chalkboard. Ask students how they propose to find the middle-sized pace. Among their suggestions, they may include ordering the tapes by size (smallest to largest, or vice versa). Try not to accept that suggestion too quickly. Wait to hear many ideas, and ask students to demonstrate or explain so that others understand their methods. When the discussion has run its course, enlist volunteer help in ordering the pace-tapes by size.

Analyzing the data: Finding the middle-sized pace

Now, how could we find the middle-sized pace?

Third and fourth graders have some good ideas about finding the middle of a set of data. Probe their ideas and question them so that their reasoning becomes clear. For an example of the discussion in one classroom, see the Dialogue Box, *Finding the middle-sized pace* (page 35).

Elena says to look for the middle. But how could we do that? Which one is in the middle? How can you tell? Can you be sure? What is the middle-sized pace?

After your class has agreed on a method, identify the middle-sized pace. Allow some time to talk about any surprises. Is the middle-sized pace very different from the others? Are the pace-lengths clumped?

Using the data: A standard pace

Now that we have agreed on the middle-sized pace, let's make copies of it with adding machine tape so that all of you can use it to measure distances in the classroom. If we measure the length of the room with the middle-sized pace, will our results vary? Let's try it.

Students may want to mark the middle-sized pace on the floor so they can practice standardizing their paces. Keeping copies of it will allow students to settle debates by referring to the tape itself. In this way the middle-sized pace will truly function as a standard measure for your class.

Set some other measuring tasks that involve pacing distances with the new standard.

Let's see how far it is to the school office in standard paces, and how far to the bathrooms. At lunchtime, see how many standard paces it takes to get to the cafeteria.

Extension: Measuring objects with the pace-tape

Students can also use the standard pace-tape as a ruler to measure objects in the classroom. They might measure things such as the teacher's desk, the chalk tray, the bulletin board, the windows—even the heights of their classmates. ■

---

66 99 DIALOGUE BOX
Finding the middle-sized pace

This discussion varies from classroom to classroom, and teachers make decisions spontaneously about what ideas to support. Because classes are so different, there is no "best" way to proceed; we include here examples from two classrooms to illustrate different approaches, both workable.

The first conversation happened after students had paced to predetermined targets in the school. They found that while the directions they wrote down worked for the one who originally paced the distance, they did not always work for the other partner. The teacher asked the students about that experience.

How many of you had the problem that your partner's paces weren't the same size as yours, so the number didn't come out right? What do you think we could do about that?

TAMARA: You can measure our paces, measure all of them, and find the biggest and the smallest and then you get the middle one and try and make everybody take that size of a pace.

BENJAMIN: The ones with the middle-sized pace come to the front of the room and walk. Then we can see who has the middle.

CHRIS: Rearrange it, the tall ones on one end, and it goes down to the other ones that way.

SAMIR: Yeah, that sounds neat!

What, Samir?

SAMIR: Like—mine, Elena's and Valerie's. Mine is smaller than Elena's and Valerie's is bigger than Elena's, we can put them in a row like that.

From smallest to largest?

SAMIR: Yeah.

How would that help us find the middle size?

TAMARA: Because the smallest one, you can start from there and go until you get to the one in the middle, and that could be the middle size.

Any other ideas to help us find the middle-sized pace?

BARBARA: I was going to measure them and then try to find the middle.

So actually write down how long the longest one was and how long the shortest one was and all the ones in between? So it's kind of the same thing, isn't it?

In this classroom the teacher expects students to give reasons for their ideas and to listen to each other so that they can relate their ideas to those of classmates. She does not force a method onto the class, but solicits methodology from them, repeating and sometimes asking questions to help them clarify and expand on their own ideas.

(Dialogue Box continued)

In a second classroom, the students did not want to select one pace as the middle one, but instead kept selecting a *range* of values as their middle. Because this was so important to them, the teacher did not push for the selection of one middle-sized pace.

During this discussion, the students were looking at a line plot that showed how many paces each of them took to cross the room.

```
                    X
                    X           X
        X   X   X       X           X   X
        X   X   X   X   X   X   X   X   X
      ─────────────────────────────────────
        12  13  14  15  16  17  18  19  20
```

JANE: These paces are the middle ones. [*Marks under 14, 15, and 16 on the chalkboard.*]

Is there one pace that's in the middle? There are 18 paces in all. Can we use that to find the middle?

SARAH: This is the middle one. [*She points to 16.*]

KEVIN: Here. 1, 2, 3, 4, 5, 6 . . . these are the big paces [*indicates 12 to 14*] and 1, 2, 3, 4, 5, 6 . . . these are the small ones [*indicates 18 to 20*] and 1, 2, 3, 4, 5, 6 . . . these are the middle ones [*indicates 15 to 17*], all six of them here.

What if we wanted to tell someone how long our middle-sized pace was?

MARIA: Just tell them in between our small-size ones and the big-size ones.

And how would we say that?

SARAH: In between here and here. [*Points to 14 and 18.*]

Can we be more specific?

JONATHAN: Say it's 17-1/2 inches, because it is.

How do you know that?

JONATHAN: It's mine and I measured it to be sure.

How do you know yours is the middle?

JONATHAN: It's in the middle group.

SARAH: But mine is too and it's shorter than yours.

☞ Most of the students really did not want to select one and only one pace for their middle-sized pace, and the teacher was willing to let them define their own terms. Like the teacher in the first classroom, she is supportive and challenging, asking students to give their reasons and explain their statements; although she makes suggestions, she lets the students set the terms of the task.

The student who had measured his own pace was unable to see that his pace might not be the only middle value in the distribution. The teacher let this go for the time being, knowing that other methods would probably appeal to him more in the long run. ■

Measuring: From Paces to Feet

PART 2
Using standard measures

ARE OUR FEET A FOOT LONG?

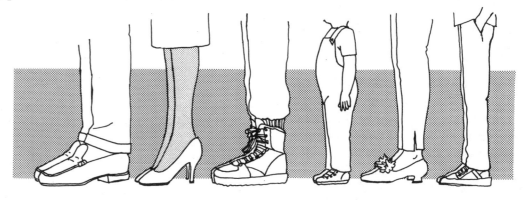

INVESTIGATION OVERVIEW

What happens

Students look for foot-long feet at home, comparing household members' feet to a foot-long measure. These data are displayed and analyzed to see how people's feet compare to a "measuring foot." In these sessions they learn an imaginary story of the development of the foot as a measure and speculate about reasons for its relatively large size.

The activities take two class sessions of about 45 minutes each.

What to plan ahead of time

▼ Obtain or prepare unmarked foot measures for each student, following the guidelines in the Teacher Note, *Rulers, footsticks, and inchsticks* (page 42).

▼ Duplicate Student Sheet 7 (page 79) for each student (Session 1).

▼ Have index cards or stick-on notes available for every student.

Important mathematical ideas

Using a standard measure. Students use an uncalibrated foot-ruler (a "footstick") to compare their feet and the feet of other people in their households. The emphasis in this investigation is on comparison with a standard (12-inch) foot. In the data collection activity, students internalize the size of the foot-ruler by using it frequently and by comparing objects with it. Rather than think of the foot as a length that is broken up into smaller pieces, we concentrate here on the foot as a unit. Support students who decide to measure other objects in addition to human feet.

Collecting, displaying, and analyzing comparative data. Students collect measurement data at home and display it at school. The combined data give them a great deal to work with, and they will need to spend time thinking about what it shows and talking about it in class. Encourage them to use sketch graphs to organize their data.

Theory-building. Third and fourth grade students often generate theories about the data they collect. Sometimes these are data-based, sometimes not. It is important that they learn to ask questions about data. What do the data tell us? What do they *not* tell us? While encouraging students to build theories, help them keep their theories grounded in the data they collect and analyze. ■

SESSION 1 ACTIVITIES

Introducing the problem: The story of the king's foot

Earlier, we measured distances—like the length of our classroom, and how far it is from our room to the front door of the school—by pacing them off. We also tried using giant steps and baby steps. Here's a story about a king who measured the same way. Listen to find out how well it worked for him.

Read the story in the box (at right) as a discussion-starter.

The King's Foot

ONCE UPON A TIME there was a king who kept ponies. His daughter, the princess, had a little pony of her own that she dearly loved. As the princess grew older she grew bigger, but the pony did not. The day came when she climbed on her pony and her feet dragged on the ground. That was the day the king decided that he would surprise his daughter with a beautiful new full-size horse.

The king went himself to the best stable in the kingdom and chose a sleek Arabian mare. "Because it's a surprise," the king said, "I want to leave the mare here at your stable until I can get a new stall built in the royal barns to fit such a grand, large horse."

The king knew that he would have to tell the royal carpenter how large to make the stall. So, using heel-to-toe baby steps, the king carefully walked around the mare. ". . . 5, 6, 7, 8, 9 feet long," he murmured, "and 3, 4, 5 feet wide." The king jotted down the numbers: 9 feet long and 5 feet wide. The message was sent to the carpenter, and she set to work at once.

Soon the stall was ready and the king sent for the mare. He thought he would have a little fun with the princess, so he had the royal groom hide the mare behind the barn. Then he said to the princess, "Come with me and see if you can guess your surprise."

Together they walked into the royal barn, past all the stalls of little ponies, and stopped in front of the empty new stall. But no sooner had the princess inspected the new stall than she burst into tears.

"I truly hoped that my surprise would be a horse, because I have outgrown my little pony. But now that I see the size of the stall, I know that you are just giving me another little pony, no larger than the first."

The king was puzzled. He saw that indeed, the new stall was much too small for a full-size horse. The groom quickly brought the new Arabian mare out of hiding, and as soon as the princess laid eyes on her, she forgot her tears. Only the king did not forget. He called angrily for the royal carpenter to account for her terrible mistake.

The carpenter was shocked. She knew she was good at her trade; her work always drew high praise. And she had made the stall just as the king had said—9 feet long and 5 feet wide. What could have happened?

[Pause and ask the students what could have happened; then continue.]

The carpenter stared sadly at her work. She paced thoughtfully around the little stall, carefully counting her foot-lengths. Then she sat down beside the king to think.

Sitting there, staring at her feet, that was when the carpenter noticed something— when she saw the king's foot next to hers. "That's it!" she cried. "Your foot is much longer than mine! I made the stall 9 feet long, but I used 9 of *my feet* instead of 9 *king's feet.*"

Then the carpenter had a truly remarkable idea. She took a flat stick of wood, and she cut it just exactly the same length as the king's foot. "This way," she told the king, "I can always know exactly how big you want things made."

Now the carpenter made a stall for the new horse that was 9 *king's feet* long and 5 *king's feet* wide. This time the stall fit perfectly. So the king was happy, and the princess was happy, and the carpenter was happiest of all. She started a factory and made lots of sticks just as long as the king's foot, which she called *rulers*. Selling these sticks, she became rich and famous.

After your reading, allow time for discussion. Some students may connect the story with their own recent measurement experiences.

Tell me again why the new stall was too small at first. How did the carpenter solve the problem? Why did she call the sticks she made "rulers"? Does this remind you of anything that's happened in the classroom? Have we had some experiences like the carpenter's?

Collecting and analyzing data: Measuring our feet

Pass out the uncalibrated foot-long rulers and explain that these "footsticks" are one official measuring foot long. After their recent experiences in measuring, students should have a solid idea about the advantages of a standard unit of measure.

Ask students to compare their own feet with these rulers and find out whether their feet are shorter than, the same length as, or longer than the ruler. Display their results on the chalkboard in a format like this:

Shorter than the foot ruler	Equal to the foot ruler	Longer than the foot ruler
Benjamin	Susan	
Shanta		
Elena		
Chris		

What do you see from these data? What can we say about your feet? Does that mean that everyone's feet are the same? What does this display tell us? What doesn't it tell us?

Collecting data at home

Do you think anyone's foot is really one foot long? Whose might be?

Third and fourth graders have feet that vary in length. Most will be less than a foot long— in fact, most adults' feet are less than a foot long. Provide time for students to speculate about whose feet might be much longer than theirs. Be sure to allow time for them to give their reasons and to talk about their ideas.

Tonight you'll be looking for a foot-long foot at home. To check foot length, you will compare everyone's foot to the foot-ruler. I'm going to give you a form for recording what you find.

Give out copies of Student Sheet 7, *Data from home: Foot size.* Explain how to use the columns to record the name and age of each person whose foot they measure. They can start by entering the data they found when they compared their own feet with the foot ruler. That is, they should write their own name and age in the appropriate column.

Extension

The history of measurement is fascinating to some students, and they may want to find out more about how our measurements have been developed and are enforced. Two Teacher Notes, *Bureau of Standards* (page 43) and *Sixteen left feet* (page 44) provide background information; you may want to share some of it with your students. ∎

Rulers, footsticks, and inchsticks

A typical school ruler can be visually confusing to many students because of the profusion of lines. When a skill is being developed or re-taught, it is important not to introduce confusing extra information. Although the usual ruler is a good tool when students understand the concept of measurement and see a need for fractional markings, the simpler the better at the beginning.

For that reason, you will need for this unit unmarked foot-long measures (footsticks) and foot measures marked in whole inches only (inchsticks). The footsticks are used in the investigation, *Are our feet a foot long?*, and the inchsticks in the investigation, *Using a smaller unit.*

Appropriate rulers are commercially available from Dale Seymour Publications. Alternatively, use the patterns on pages 80–81 to make your own. A 9-by-12-inch piece of tagboard can be cut into nine footsticks. Inch-square graph paper is useful for making inchsticks. When laminated, these rulers can be used over and over.

The footsticks were named by a fourth grader who enjoyed the fact that they were exactly one foot long, and that he could tell immediately whether something was longer or shorter than a foot. Indeed, this footstick makes simple comparison much easier. When your students measure and compare the lengths of human feet, both in class and at home, they can make a simple "shorter/longer/equal to" comparison without the distraction of the inch-marks on a typical ruler. You can help your students internalize the length of a foot by using the footsticks to measure a variety of objects in the classroom after finishing this *Used Numbers* unit.

Similarly, when inchsticks were used in one third grade class, the students found they could easily tell the lengths of objects by counting inch-squares on the inchsticks. They were relieved not to have the "extra" lines found on the school ruler, and the alternating colors of the inch squares made counting even easier. Fractional parts of an inch were introduced gradually, as needed, when the teacher felt that students were ready. Working with whole inches before introducing fractions gave students a firm base for their understanding of measurement. Gradually they came to see that halves and fourths of an inch sometimes add useful information.

We encourage you to keep the measurement tools simple at the start so that they engage all the students in your class. The National Council of Teachers of Mathematics' *Curriculum and Evaluation Standards* (Reston, VA: 1989) suggests that teachers observe students' work in mathematics in order to learn what they know and how they think about mathematics. The measurement activities in this unit allow you to engage your students in conversations that will help you to assess their measurement skills in a real context. As they work, talking with small groups about the task and their approaches to it will give you a great deal of valuable observational information. Keep an eye out for the students who can easily handle the more sophisticated tools as well as those who are struggling. You will find that the knowledge you gain from these observations will help you to plan follow-up measurement activities. ■

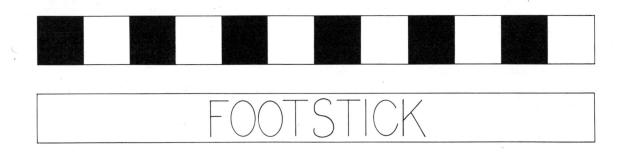

✎ TEACHER NOTE
Bureau of Standards: Home of the official U.S. measures

☛ This background information is provided for your interest; share it with your class as you deem appropriate.

The Bureau of Standards in Washington, DC, sets the standards that regulate measurements. Within the bureau, the Division of Weights and Measures regulates all the measurements used in trade—pounds, meters, kilograms, yards, gallons, and so forth.

If there is a disagreement about the amounts being weighed or measured, the people who disagree can seek help from the Division of Weights and Measures in their own state. The federal office coordinates the states and enforces interstate regulations. The goal is to make sure that items sold (ranging from fuel oil to oatmeal) meet the packaging standards set by the Division.

In order to enforce the law, there has to be a place to settle disagreements about what a pound *really* weighs. At one time, physical models of the official yard, foot, and pound were all kept at the Bureau of Standards, so that various measuring devices could be "set" against them. These measures were housed in special vaults at the Bureau. Copies of them were found in the Museum of the National Institute of Standards.

Now, however, all linear measurements based on the yard have been calibrated to the meter. Even though our country has not entirely converted to the metric system, the yard is now measured in metric terms. And although there is a physical model of a meter bar (the Official Meter) at the Bureau of Standards, the meter is actually defined in terms of the speed of light! That is, a meter is the distance light travels in a vacuum in 1/300 millionth of a second. Clearly we've moved a long way from the original, time-honored measurements based on the body.

Weights are still kept at the Bureau as physical models, so it is possible to see the Official Kilogram. Just as the yard is now measured in terms of the meter, the pound is calibrated to the kilogram. It is ironic that we claim not to be converting to the metric system when our English measures are now determined metrically.

The history of weights and measures includes many interesting tidbits. For example, Napoleon mandated the metric system because it was more systematic and scientific than the body-based systems used in France. Its abstraction and rationality fit perfectly with the growth of rational science at that time in history.

English measures, too, have an interesting history. Your students may want to write for information about the history of weights and measures in the United States. Address such requests to National Institute of Standards and Technology, Office of Weights and Measures, Room A-617, Gaithersburg, MD 20899; phone (301) 975-2000. ■

EXHIBIT ROOM
Bureau of Standards

FIRST OFFICIAL INCH

FIRST OFFICIAL FOOT

FIRST OFFICIAL YARD

Sixteen left feet

Although people have been measuring in one way or another for many thousands of years, the use of *standard* measurement is relatively recent when all of human history is taken into account. That is, measures have been standardized only in the last two thousand years. Measurements were originally based in the human body and became standardized when people needed a clearer way to communicate their results (often, because they were written down and sent to different places). For example, directions for cooking once relied on "handfuls" and "pinches," but these have evolved into "cups" and "teaspoons"—measures whose volume is specified and standardized.

Measures of length have likewise evolved standards that are not subject to human variability. In this excerpt from an old encyclopedia, you can get a flavor of the problems of living in a non-standardized world (and some of its joys!):

A good idea of the inconvenience caused by the lack of absolute and invariable standards is furnished by a German treatise on surveying of the 16th century, which instructs the surveyor to establish the length of a rood thus: "Stand at the door of a church on a Sunday and bid 16 men to stop, tall ones and small ones, as they happen to pass out when the service is finished; then make them put
*their left feet one behind the other, and the length thus obtained shall be a right and lawful rood to measure and survey the land with, and the 16th part of it shall be a right and lawful foot." **

Your students may want to explore the length of their own *rood* and compare theirs with another class's *rood*. How much variation in result is there if they choose sixteen students by drawing names from hats? Fourth graders particularly might want to play with some of these possibilities.

If you have students who are particularly interested in history, the history of measurements opens a real door to the past. They may want to look up other early definitions of measures. How did the "foot" as we know it evolve, really? How was an acre defined? Many encyclopedias offer information on the evolution of measurements. ■

---

*From *Compton's Pictured Encyclopedia*, 1929 edition. Chicago: F.E. Compton & Company. We are grateful to Margaret W. Maxfield of Kansas State University, whose article "Sixteen Left Feet" in *The Best of Teaching Statistics*, Peter Holmes, ed. (Sheffield, England: Teaching Statistics Trust, 1986), brought this to our attention.

SESSION 2 ACTIVITIES

Recording the homework data: Foot sizes

Ask how many students found a foot-long foot at home. Count the number and ask whose feet those were.

We're going to be putting all our data together so we can compare everyone's results at once. You need to make a card for each person whose feet you measured.

Students write the name and age of each person whose foot they measured on a stick-on note or an index card. If some students have measured a lot of people, those who measured fewer can help them record all the names and ages. While students are doing this, replicate the columns of Student Sheet 7 on the board.

Shorter than the foot ruler	Equal to the foot ruler	Longer than the foot ruler
Shawn 4	Tara 17	Daddy 34
Janie 12		Rolf 24

Students then stick each name card in the correct column on the board, showing whether the feet they measured are shorter than, the same length as, or longer than a foot ruler.

Describing the data: Looking at the display

Count the number in each category. Ask

student pairs to discuss the chart together and to make a statement about what this chart shows them and what it doesn't show. Ask the pairs to share their statements with the class. Some students may have powerful beliefs about what they can see from these data. (See the Dialogue Box, *Measuring feet: Are older feet bigger feet?*, page 46.)

The next step may be to tally the results. If you think it would be helpful to your students, replace each card with a tally mark in the appropriate column. You could use this opportunity to demonstrate the convention for tallying by fives (JHT).

Analyzing the data: What do we know about foot size?

What can we tell from these data? Are there any surprises? Are there any patterns? Do you see anything you consider unusual?

Encourage students to talk about what they see in this collection of data. Some have commented on the large number of people in the "smaller than a foot" section. Others have generated theories about foot growth.

This discussion can go in many different directions. Your students' theories and ideas may surprise you!

Extensions

Some students may want to conduct more research and collect more data about foot

size. Is there another group whose feet they might measure? They may be interested in some tall people's foot sizes.

Robert Pershing Wadlow, the world's tallest man at 8 feet 11.1 inches, wore size 37AA shoes. His feet were 18-1/2 inches long.

Zeng Jinlian, the world's tallest woman, had 14-inch-long feet.

These facts come from the *Guinness Book of World Records*, edited by Alan Russell and Norris McWhirter (New York: Bantam Books, 1988). ■

❝❞DIALOGUE BOX
Measuring feet: Are older feet bigger feet?

This third grade class has brought in a great deal of data from home. They compared people's feet with the footsticks and have recorded each person's foot as longer than, shorter than, or equal to one foot. They have spent time putting their data together. Here is a partial table of their results. (Note that they actually looked at a huge display of all the names and ages of the people they measured, and then counted to find the totals.)

Foot length	Total	Name and age
shorter than a foot	74	Jamie 3, Peggy 10, Bobby 9, Sean 9, Mom 27, . . .
equal to a foot	21	Benjamin 11, Joseph 18, Serena 37, . . .
longer than a foot	33	Dad 34, Grampy 67, Bobby's brother 19, . . .

The teacher wants to see what the students find in these data.

Do you have comments about these results?

MICHAEL: We measured 128 people in all.

How do you get that number?

MICHAEL: I added 74 and 21 and 33.

TAMARA: I'm surprised that there are more people in the "longer than a foot" group than in the "same as a foot" group.

Me, too.

SHANTA: But the ones that are older have bigger feet.

BENJAMIN: But the *oldest* person has the *smallest* foot.

SU-MEI: When you are in the middle of your age you have the biggest foot.

RAY: Whenever you get older and the body stops growing, the foot stops growing.

BARBARA: When you're young, your foot is short; when you're in the middle, your foot is longer; and when you're older, your foot is shorter.

RICARDO: The body never stops growing. It makes new cells all the time, and that makes it grow. Making cells makes it grow.

So what do you think happens to your foot size?

RICARDO: It's still growing but it just doesn't show that it's growing.

OK, so how do you feel about this category? Where would you fit when you were real old?

KIM: In "longer than a foot."

Let me ask you all a question. Could we have real old people in every category?

SEVERAL STUDENTS: Yeah, you could.

☞ In this discussion, students are expressing their ideas about relationships between age and foot size. Even though some of the ideas sound very strange to adults, the teacher allows the students to talk about them. Her final question helps students focus their ideas and allows them to look at a new question in this context. The misconceptions about growth and foot size are tabled, as the teacher decides to deal with them in a later science lesson. ∎

USING A SMALLER UNIT

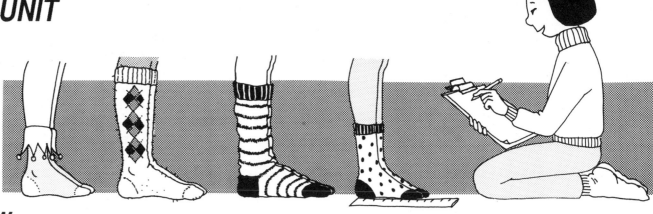

INVESTIGATION OVERVIEW

What happens

Students establish a method for measuring their feet in inches, then analyze the data to decide on a typical foot length for their class. They compare their class data with data on the foot lengths of teachers in their school and describe the differences in these distributions. In order to practice using inches to measure objects longer than one foot, they measure their heights in inches and find the height of the middle-sized third [fourth] grader.

The activities take four class sessions of about 45 minutes each.

What to plan ahead of time

▼ Prepare inchsticks (see page 81) or provide rulers calibrated in whole inches for every student (Sessions 1 and 2).

Avoid using rulers with half- and quarter-inch marks, since those are confusing to many students at this age level.

▼ The day before Session 1, remind students to wear clean socks the next day because they will be measuring their feet with shoes off.

▼ Provide blank paper and pencils to use for sketch graphs (Session 1).

▼ Before Session 2, make arrangements with the other teachers in your school so that your students can come to them to measure their feet. You might make a schedule for your students' visits and double-check it with the faculty.

▼ After you have a line plot of the data students collect in Session 1, make copies for small-group work (Session 2).

▼ Provide material for making presentation graphs, including graph paper, construction paper, stick-on dots, markers, scissors (Sessions 2 and 3).

▼ Have available adding machine tape, scissors, yardsticks, or measuring tapes (Session 4).

Important mathematical ideas

Measuring with inches as a standard. Students use calibrated rulers for more accurate measures of foot length as they practice using inches as a measurement unit.

Measuring objects shorter and longer than the foot-ruler, and specifying lengths in small units. Objects smaller than a ruler can be measured more easily than those that are larger; with a small object, students can simply line up the end of the ruler with the end of the object and read off the number on the ruler at the other end of the object. They can do this mechanically, without an understanding of what these numbers mean. Being specific about a length that is longer than a foot involves re-placing the ruler, adding totals, and understanding the relationship of inches to feet. Repeated repositioning of the ruler echoes the iterative movements of the pacing students did to measure distances in earlier investigations.

Collecting and analyzing data to find what's typical of a data set. Students define their methods, collect data, and display them, looking for ways to describe the typical foot lengths in their class. As they look for ways to describe these data, they develop a more extensive vocabulary for data description, including ways to define what's typical of those data.

Developing methods of displaying and comparing data. Students first display one set of data—their foot lengths—and find the typical foot length (for their class) in inches. Next they display and compare these results with teachers' foot lengths. They draw from previous experiences to develop techniques for comparing sets of data. ∎

SESSION 1 ACTIVITIES

Exploring a new tool: The inchstick

You've compared your feet with a foot-ruler and most of you found that your foot is not a foot long. So we know that your foot is shorter than a foot—but just how long is it? How could we find out? The rulers you'll be using today are marked off in inches, which have been used for hundreds of years to measure things. An inch is about the same size as the first joint on your thumb.

Pass out the inchsticks or rulers. Encourage students to find their own personal benchmarks corresponding to one foot or one inch (see the Teacher Note, *Benchmarks on the body*, page 50). They can record this information as a group by making two posters: *Benchmarks: One foot long* and *Benchmarks: One inch long*. Another way to record the information is to give students index cards for writing down their personal benchmarks. Students might illustrate their personal measurements to keep for future reference.

Ask students to try using their benchmarks to measure some small things: a pencil, a paper clip, an index card, a pocket. They can then use inchsticks to check. If your students get answers that are between two inchmarks, you may want to discuss what to do.

If it's between 3 inches and 4 inches, you might pick the number it's closest to. If it's

about halfway, you may call it 3-1/2. It's all right to approximate.**

Collecting data: Deciding how to measure our feet

Now we're going to use inches to measure our feet. We'll write down everyone's results to see what we can learn about foot size in our class.

Scientists collect data from measuring things, and sometimes they have to redo a whole experiment because different people measured things in different ways. Let's make some decisions about how we'll measure.

Should we measure with our shoes on or off? Would it make any difference? Where should we put the ruler? Should we stand up or sit down while we're measuring? Would that make a difference? What if the length is a little more than an inch-measure? Should we round down, round up, or use fractional parts of an inch?

Encourage students to try a variety of methods to see how their results for the same foot differ according to the method used. Give them a chance to talk about what they think gives a reasonable measure of foot length. Help them decide how to make the measurement standard for everyone. Write their agreed-on methods on the board for reference.

Ask students to measure their feet again, following the established method, and write their results on a stick-on note or index card.

Displaying and describing the data: What do we see in the data?

Record their results on the board as a simple, unordered list:

7 inches

9 inches

8 inches

$9\frac{1}{2}$ inches

8 inches

We're trying to find what the typical foot length is in our class—but looking at all these numbers, it's hard to tell what would be typical. If we wanted to organize these numbers better, how could we do it?

Working in pairs or small groups, students make sketch graphs to organize the data, showing the distribution of foot lengths in the classroom. These need not be painstaking, but can be quite sketchy. Think of them as first draft graphs (for details, see the Teacher Note, *Sketch graphs: Easy to make, quick to read*, page 50).

When they have finished making their sketch graphs, ask them to think about what the graphs show, and write one sentence about their sketch graphs on the same sheet of paper. When every pair is done, call them together for a discussion.

Finding patterns in the data: What's typical of our feet?

What's typical of your feet? How can we say what we see? Are there clumps or clusters of data? Are there any outliers? What else can you tell me about the lengths of your feet?

Discussing what they see in their sketch graphs may provide the opportunity to review statistical terms. Refer to the Teacher Note, *Statistical words to introduce as appropriate* (page 33).

Looking at our data, what would you say is the length of a typical third [fourth] grader's foot?

This discussion requires the teacher to be flexible, yet it is important that students' misconceptions be addressed. This is a delicate balance. As students talk about what they think is typical, you will hear many different theories and many reasons. Some students will choose the mode (the most frequent). Some will look for a range of values. Some will find a middle value (the median). For typical problems that arise, see the two Dialogue Boxes, *Describing data: Getting caught in the range* (page 51) and *Discussing invented methods for finding typical values* (page 54).

It is important to help students sort out methods and answers that seem sensible and for which they have strong reasons.

Although no answer is "wrong," some answers are more typical of this distribution than are others.

When the students have reached some conclusions about typical foot length in the class, write these down and keep them with the data for use in the next session. Remember to duplicate the data for small-group work, and to speak with your colleagues to find good times to measure their feet.

Extensions

If time allows and you want to continue the activity, ask students what shoe size they wear (those who don't know may be able to find it inside their shoes). Compare the distribution of foot length with the distribution of shoe size. Are they identical? What might explain some differences?

You might also ask students whether they can make a rule about the relationship between foot length and shoe size. This provides good practice in finding and describing number patterns. ∎

✎ TEACHER NOTE
Benchmarks on the body

Carpenters used to make marks on their workbenches to indicate lengths that they often used—such as 2 inches, or 4 inches, or 1 foot. These "benchmarks" speeded up the measuring process, since the carpenter did not then need to find a measuring tape or ruler every time. In a similar way, "benchmarks" on the body are useful because we often need to estimate measurements when we don't have a ruler handy.

You can help your students find such benchmarks; for instance, an inch is about the size of the first joint on the thumb. Ask students to check this out with their inchsticks and see if it's true for them. They can use the footsticks to find a place on the body that is 1 foot long. One possibility is the forearm. Or, they may find something—like a handspan—that measures 6 inches; two of these would equal 1 foot.

Teachers who have done this—had students find benchmarks on their bodies and then use those benchmarks to estimate other lengths—have found that it helps their students internalize the measures. They are able to estimate measurements with reference to their own bodies and no longer feel the need to rely on a ruler all the time. One third grade teacher overhead his students giving each other directions to pour water into a glass. The first student asked,

"How full?" and the second responded, while looking at her thumb, "About two inches."

Once benchmarks on the body are established, it's important to *use* these measurements as much as possible every day in school. Teachers have found ways to weave measurement into lining up for recess ("Everyone whose little finger is less than 3 inches can line up now"), selecting students for special jobs ("Anyone with a handspan of more than 7 inches can help here"), or doing tasks at the end of the school day ("Find an object that's between 5 and 6 inches long and put it away"). If you have your students first estimate with their benchmarks and later use a ruler to check their estimates, you will be helping them internalize a system of measurement. That skill will help them tremendously, both in mathematics classes and in their daily lives. ■

✎ TEACHER NOTE
Sketch graphs: Quick to make, easy to read

Graphing is often taught as an art of presentation, as the endpoint of the data analysis process, as the means for communicating what has been found. Certainly, a pictorial representation is an effective way to present data to an audience at the end of an investigation. But graphs, tables, diagrams, and charts are also data analysis tools. A user of statistics employs pictures and graphs frequently *during the process of analysis* as a means of better understanding the data.

Many working graphs need never be shown to anyone else or posted on the wall. Students can make and use them just to help uncover the story of the data. We call such representations used during the process of data analysis "sketch graphs" or "rough draft graphs."

```
6  ✓                    10
7  ✓ ✓ ✓             9  9  9  9
8  ✓ ✓                8  8
9  ✓ ✓ ✓ ✓           7  7  7
10 ✓                    6
```

We want students to become comfortable with a variety of such working graphs. Sketch graphs should be easy to make and easy to read; they should not challenge students' patience or fine motor skills. Unlike graphs for presentation, sketch graphs do not require neatness, careful measurement or scaling, use of clear titles or labels, or decorative work.

Sketch graphs:

▼ can be made rapidly

▼ reveal aspects of the shape of the data

▼ are clear, but not necessarily neat

▼ don't require labels or titles (as long as students are clear about what they are looking at)

▼ don't require time-consuming attention to color or design

Encourage students to invent different forms until they discover some that work well in organizing their data. Sketch graphs might be made with pencil and paper, with Unifix or other connecting cubes, or with stick-on notes. Cubes and stick-on notes offer flexibility because they can easily be rearranged.

```
        X              6 □
   X    X              7 □□□
   X  X  X             8 □□
 X  X  X  X  X         9 □□□□
 ─────────────
 6  7  8  9  10       10 □
```

One standard form of representation that is particularly useful for a first look at the data—the line plot—is suggested for use throughout this unit. ■

❝❞DIALOGUE BOX
Describing data: Getting caught in the range

These students have just finished measuring the length of their feet in inches. Their collection of data looks like this:

9 10 7 9 9 8 9 8 8 9
9 $9\frac{1}{2}$ 9 6 10 $10\frac{1}{2}$

To organize the data, they decide to make a line plot.

```
                        X
                        X
                        X
                        X
              X         X
              X         X         X
 X     X      X      X  X  X  X
 ──────────────────────────────
 6     7      8      9  9½ 10  10½
```

Looking at the shape of the data, they observe that it has a range from 6 to 10-1/2 inches, that most of the data are around 8 or 9 inches (a clump), and that almost half the feet are 9 inches long. At this point they begin to focus on finding the typical foot, which they decide is the middle-sized foot.

How can we find the middle-sized foot from using this line plot?

SAMIR: It's 9, because most of the people have 9.

Why do you say 9 is the middle size?

SAMIR: There are seven of those [marks above the 9] and seven of the numbers on the number line, three on this side and three on that side, so 9 is right in the middle.

VALERIE: I was thinking that 6 was in the middle.

Why do you think that?

VALERIE: Because if you count from 1 to 10, 6 is in the middle.

Does it matter to you that there are more marks above the 9 than above the 6?

VALERIE: No. I'm just looking at the numbers and it doesn't matter if there are more marks above one number than above the other.

PEGGY: How can it be 6? 'Cuz 6 is way down at the *least* part, it's the *last* one, and the line goes to 10-1/2, so *how* can 6 be in the middle? So 6 is the *lowest* we have in the class, not the middle.

I'm curious about some of your ways to find the middle-sized foot. Let's try something to help me understand. Would it change things if we showed the data this way?

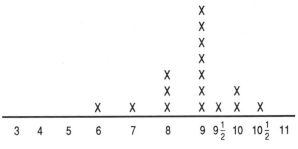

(Dialogue Box continued)

Does this change your ideas about how big the middle-sized foot is?

CHRIS: Yes. It's 8 now because that's the middle number. Three matches with 11 and 4 with 10-1/2, and 5 with 10, and 6 with 9-1/2, and 7 with 9, and that leaves 8 in the middle.

ELENA: No, I don't agree. We don't have people at 3 and 4 and 5 and 11. And there's lots of people at 9. So I think it's really more like 9.

Well, we seem to have a lot of controversy. I think it's important for you to think about whether we're looking for a middle *number* or a middle-sized *foot*. Which one were we looking for?

RAY: The middle-sized foot.

Then it's important for us to think about how to do that. What did we do when we found the middle-sized pace?

MICHAEL: We put them in order and we found the ones in the middle.

Can we do something like that here?

☞ This teacher is trying to lead students away from looking only at the number line and the *range* of numbers on it. Many in the class don't understand how to find the middle from looking at the graph (it may be that this idea develops fairly slowly over time). The teacher realizes that they are caught in the range, the numbers along the bottom of the graph. It is difficult for students to ignore the compelling, simple list of numerals along the bottom and to focus instead on the overall distribution of data displayed *above* those numbers. To help them, this teacher shifted gears, and the class ended up putting their foot lengths in order from shortest to longest foot, finding the middle foot in the list, and calling that the middle-sized foot.

This teacher was aware that students had ideas to be shared, but she was not afraid to push the students beyond what they initially believed. This combination of sensitivity and willingness to challenge often seems to produce the most thought-provoking class discussions. ■

SESSION 2 AND 3 ACTIVITIES

Posing the question: How much longer are teachers' feet than ours?

Remind students about the conclusions they reached in their last session about the typical foot length of members of this class.

Today we'll be comparing your feet with another group of feet to see how the lengths are similar and different. You said that the way you'd describe the typical foot length in our class was [9 inches]. Do you think the teachers' feet in this school will be much longer or shorter than yours? What would you predict? Do you have an estimate of the length of a middle-sized teacher-foot?

Collect and record students' estimates of typical teacher foot length. Ask for some of their reasons.

Collecting data: Measuring teachers' feet

What data do we need to collect to answer our question? How can we collect those data to find out?

Generate ideas from the class fairly quickly. They will need to specify a method before collecting data, and they may want to do as they did when they measured their own foot-lengths.

Share your data collection schedule so that

students know when to measure teachers' feet. Select and determine teams to measure and collect data. As students return, help them to consolidate their results.

Organizing and displaying data: How long is a typical teacher's foot?

You may want to talk about ways of finding out what's typical. See the Dialogue Box, *Discussing invented methods for finding typical values* (page 54) for some ideas.

Put all the teachers' foot length data up on the board. Ask students to organize it to look for patterns. Compare methods and then ask students to describe the typical teacher's foot length. Think about clumps and clusters of data, and whether there are some clear patterns.

Analyzing the data: Comparing teachers' feet and students' feet

How can we compare these two sets of data? We have the data on teachers' feet now, and you have the data on your feet. Can you think of ways of comparing these data? Your task in small groups is to find some ways of comparing these data sets and answering the question, "How much longer are teachers' feet than ours?"

Students can invent some wonderful comparative techniques! Some will want to compare medians—others will compare line plots

or bar graphs. This is not easy work. Making decisions about how to display and how to compare two data sets is very complex. Allow a good deal of time for students to talk about their ideas, to share their data displays, and to draw some conclusions in their small groups (see the Teacher Note, *Phases of data analysis*, page 65).

As you circulate among the groups, ask students questions about their methods and their reasons. Bring their focus back to the question of comparison when you think it is needed. Help them relate their displays of data to their conclusions. You may need to spend time asking groups to tell you what their displays show, because some lose track of the whole picture as they begin to display the details.

Ask groups to share their conclusions and their data displays informally. Help them see where their ideas are similar and where they are different. It may help to ask questions designed to probe their understanding

What if we added a class of kindergarteners? How would you show their feet too? What kind of results would you expect?

Extensions

Your students may be interested in making a giant chart displaying the foot size in one class at each grade level in the school, or in comparing high school students with themselves. Some may want to talk with shoe store personnel about the distribution of foot size in the adult population. ■

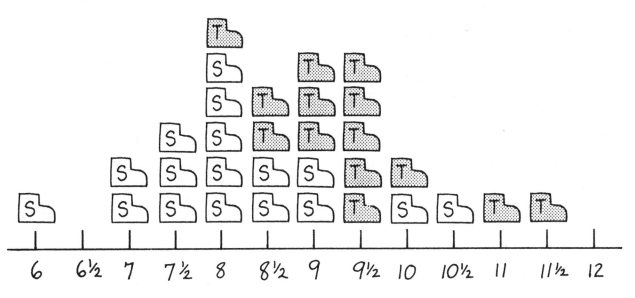

Discussing invented methods for finding typical values

```
        X
        X           X   X   X
        X           X   X   X           X
X       X   X   X   X   X           X
X       X   X   X   X   X   X   X
8  8½   9  9½  10  10½  11  11½  12
```

So, looking at these data, how can we find the typical length of a teacher's foot?

CHRIS: We think you should pick a number that comes up the most, so we got 9 inches, because more teachers had 9-inch feet than any other number.

What does everyone else think about that method?

VALERIE: We did the same thing. There are a lot of 9s, so that seemed like what was typical.

Did anybody make a different choice?

JENNIFER: We came out with 10-1/2.

So your choice is a little higher than what Chris's group picked. Why do you think that's reasonable?

SU-MEI: I don't know. It just seemed like that would be it.

But I'm interested in your reason for 10-1/2. [Pause. Still no response from the student.] **I see a big clump of data between 10 and 11 inches.**

SU-MEI: Yeah, the clump seems like it's crowded around 10-1/2.

Yes, that's an interesting reason. I can see your reasons for both of these methods. Does anyone have a good argument for choosing one over the other for the most typical value for the teachers' feet?

BOBBY: Well, even though 9 inches has the most, there are still only five teachers with 9, but there are 12 teachers bunched around 10, 10-1/2, and 11.

So you'd choose the biggest clump of data?

[Later in the same discussion] . . .

BARBARA: Our group chose 12.

What were your reasons?

BARBARA: A lot of teachers had 12, and also it's the highest number.

You chose the highest number?

BARBARA: Yes, because a bunch of teachers had it.

What do some of you who picked numbers around 9 or 10 inches think about that?

JENNIFER: I don't think you should pick the highest, because that's not like what's typical. Most teachers don't have feet that big.

CHRIS: Yeah, like with our paces, the typical pace wasn't the shortest or the longest, but somewhere in the middle.

So you think a middle value is more typical. What do you think about that argument, Ben?

BENJAMIN: Yeah, but maybe more people really have 12. We didn't measure all the teachers in the school.

So you're asking a new question: If you measured more teachers' feet, would more of them come out around 12 inches?

BENJAMIN: Yeah.

Ben noticed that four teachers had 12-inch feet; that's an important part of the shape of these data. But Chris and Michael are arguing that with these data, a *typical* value wouldn't be that high.

JEREMY: But can we try measuring Mr. Crane and Mr. Diaz? They're both really tall.

☞ This kind of discussion can be a difficult one for the teacher because while there is certainly not a single right answer, students may come up with unreasonable approaches. Encourage students' invented methods; many of their ideas will lead to understanding the idea of choosing a reasonable typical value and will prepare them for later work with standard measures of center, such as median and mode. However, students should not get the message that any method is as good as any other; expect students to reflect on whether or not their results are reasonable. Juxtaposing one student method with another, as the teacher does in this discussion, is often a good way to help students think about the reasonableness of their own methods. ∎

SESSION 4 ACTIVITIES

Considering the problem: Finding the middle-sized third [fourth] grader

We've been measuring foot length in inches. Could we use inches to measure our height as well? How many inches tall do you think you are? Could we figure out how many inches tall a typical third [fourth] grader is? How could we do that?

Allow time for a discussion of this idea. They'll be measuring in inches—how can they do that? Can they connect this task with any other measurement problems they have worked on? Will they use the same procedures?

Collecting data: Measuring our own heights

Let's figure out what procedures we could use to measure how tall you are.

Students may find that measuring height is more difficult than they had anticipated (see the Teacher Note, *Measuring heights: Using tools*, page 56). Some methods that students have used successfully are as follows:

▼ Stand with your back against the chalkboard and have a friend make a mark where the top of your head is, then measure up the wall.

▼ Stand against the wall and have a friend hold a pencil where the top of your head comes; then measure up the wall.

▼ Lie down and have a friend mark where your feet and head are; then measure the distance between those two marks.

Many confusions about standard measures will surface when students are measuring distances longer than the ruler being used. The Dialogue Box, *I'm 48 inches and 1 centimeter tall!* (page 57), offers some ideas for handling typical misunderstandings.

Displaying data: What can we say about our heights?

Draw a line plot on the chalkboard to organize and display the data. As you set it up, ask students to talk you through the process: they should establish the range, and tell you what values to write below the number line. Have them put their data on the line plot themselves.

As they put their data on the board, encourage students to make predictions. What will the shortest height be? The tallest? The middle-sized height?

Now, let's talk about the heights of the third [fourth] graders in this room. What can you see from our display? Do you see any clusters? What's the middle of the data?

What can you say about your heights from this display? What doesn't this display tell you?

Reporting on the data: Writing conclusions

After a discussion of their findings, have students work in pairs to write the story of these data. Some may want to draw their classmates; others may want to write a pen-pal letter describing their heights. Some students may want to include foot data as well. Ask them to make a display of the data on their paper, and to write some sentences that describe their conclusions and observations. Think of the graph as the picture that prompts the story, and ask students to tell as much as they can about the overall shape of the data.

When these stories are finished, give students a chance to share them, perhaps through oral reports, or a bulletin board display, or a class booklet of the collected stories. ■

✎ TEACHER NOTE
Measuring heights: Using tools

Measuring heights seems simple enough, but for elementary students it can pose a real challenge. Even though students can do measurement worksheets and manipulate measurement data on paper, they may not have had much experience using rulers and other measurement tools. Students who have done woodworking, who have built things at home, who have played with and built models (including dollhouses) will be the most expert at this activity. They have some physical experience to draw from—they are familiar with tools and know how to use them, and they may have internalized the sizes of the measurement units.

Conducting measurement activities in small groups allows you to take the observer's role, to see what understandings and misconceptions your students have. Listening to their comments and questions as you circulate will give you some real insight into the mechanical and conceptual problems that measurement often presents to them.

Some predictable problems arise when students use measurement tools. The need to line up the ruler at zero is not always obvious. Additionally, students may start from the wrong end when they pick up and move a ruler. They may combine units, using both metric and English systems. They may not notice that their "yardstick" is a meterstick.

All these skills depend to some degree on prior measurement experience.

For many teachers, it helps to think of students' initial measurements as *first approximations* to their answers, rather than final results. A vital part of their learning is the opportunity to discuss the reasonableness of their measurements, to measure several times, and to correct their measuring mistakes. When students feel the results matter, they become much more precise.

A teacher's role in this process is delicate. Your students will need to discuss their methods (Should they use the yardstick? the foot ruler? Should they stand against the wall?) as well as talking about their results. Asking questions that focus on whether their results make sense (Is Jeremy about the same height as Elena? Is Su-Mei that much taller than Susan?) will help students think about what their results mean.

Measurement work provides a natural place to use the calculator. If some students measure in inches and others in feet and inches, you have a good opportunity to work with conversion methods. Although conversion seems straightforward to adults, it is hard work for elementary students. Students will have a variety of methods and will want to spend some time trying them out. Be sure that they estimate first, so that they can check the calculator results with common sense. This step will further reinforce the role of estimation in the measurement process. ■

I'm 48 inches and 1 centimeter tall!

During this investigation, you will probably discover that many students have difficulty with linear measurement. Teachers commonly find that some of their upper elementary students:

▼ combine metric and English systems ("I'm 48 inches and 1 centimeter tall.")

▼ do not distinguish between metric and English units ("I'm 125 inches tall.")

▼ do not know how to combine two parts of the measurement ("I'm 6 inches taller than one yardstick—how do I do that?")

▼ measure from the wrong end of the ruler or yardstick

Don't be alarmed! Such difficulties are common among students who have had little experience with measurement in a real context. Use this investigation as an opportunity for students to gain experience and to help each other be accurate. Having students discuss and check accuracy as they work in small groups is often more effective than teaching a lesson on linear measurement. Have students share the difficulties they encounter; support students who use their own experience and knowledge to check the reasonableness of their measurements.

This dialogue occurred in a fifth grade class doing another *Used Numbers* unit, *Statistics: The shape of the data.* However, it highlights issues that are likely to occur when third and fourth graders try to measure their heights.

What were some of the problems you noticed in trying to get accurate measurements of your height?

SARAH: Well, in our group we got 50 inches for Mary, and then we got 125 inches for Karen, and we knew that didn't make any sense because Karen and Mary are about the same.

KAREN: And, anyway, no one could be 125 inches!

SUE: Yeah, that would be past the ceiling. [Laughter.]

I'm not sure it would be past the ceiling, but you're right—it doesn't sound like a fifth grader! So you paid attention to whether your measurements seemed reasonable. Before you tell us what was wrong, can anyone else guess how they got 125 inches for someone's height?

DAVE: I know, because we did the same thing. Because on one side is centimeters and on one side is inches, and we were using the centimeter side at first. Then we realized it couldn't be over 100 inches for somebody's height.

Is Dave right? Was that the problem?

ROBERTO: Yeah, we got confused about the two sides of the yardstick.

Anyone else come up with a problem they had to solve when they were measuring?

JANE: Yeah, we did. We measured me and we came out to 57 inches, and I *know* I'm not 57 inches.

How did you know?

JANE: Because my mom keeps a chart at home of all the kids and we mark it on our birthdays, and I know I'm shorter than that. On my birthday I was 51.

KIM: And also Jane's one of the shortest in our class, and 57 wouldn't be near to the shortest height in the class.

So you realized that 57 inches wasn't reasonable? Did you figure out what happened?

JANE: Yeah. When we measured the first part and then we moved the ruler up to measure the rest, we flipped it around and we had the ruler going in the wrong direction.

Oh, you mean you measured from the end of the yardstick that says 36?

KIM: Yeah, we got to 36 and then we swung it around like this, so we were measuring from 36 *up*, and we marked the second part at 21, so we had 36 plus 21 inches and we got 57. But we were going the wrong way. ■

Measuring: From Paces to Feet

PART 3

A project in data analysis

A note on the final projects

Two final projects are suggested here. You may do both, but most teachers have selected the one that best fits their situation and the interests of their students.

The first project focuses on classroom furniture, using measurement to analyze whether the classroom furniture fits the students and making recommendations about the optimal distribution of chairs and desks for the class. If your students are interested in measurement as a tool to analyze their own sizes (which will have emerged in the foot-size and height investigations), this investigation will be very appealing.

The second investigation uses data collected *outside* of the classroom. Students try to get measurements of the "comfort distance" for pigeons, or some other ubiquitous neighborhood animal. They work in teams, getting as close to a pigeon as they can before it flies off, then measuring the distance and recording it. The data are recorded and analyzed, and students look for patterns to see whether they can make assertions about pigeons' comfort distance. This has been appealing to students who are particularly interested in animal behavior, and it sparks many students' interest in interdisciplinary science work. ■

CLASSROOM FURNITURE: DO OUR CHAIRS FIT US?

INVESTIGATION OVERVIEW

What happens

In this investigation students explore whether their chairs fit their bodies. After hearing the story of *Goldilocks and the Three Bears*, they determine how they might measure themselves and their chairs: Which body dimensions affect the fit? They establish what methods of measurement to use; then they measure themselves and the chairs in the classroom. Finally, they write a letter to the principal about their findings.

The activities take three class sessions of about 45 minutes each.

What to plan ahead of time

▼ Prepare to read "Goldilocks and the Three Bears" (Session 1). We provide an adapted version that stresses size as a criterion of how well a chair fits (see the Teacher Note, *Goldilocks and the three*

bears, page 66). If you prefer to use your own version, be aware that for this investigation, it is important to stress *size* rather than hardness or softness for determining chair comfort.

▼ Have on hand chairs of three sizes: one very small, one very large, and one "just right" for your students (Session 1).

▼ Have adding machine tape, scissors, pencils, and yardsticks available (Sessions 1 and 2).

▼ Duplicate a class list for each small group to use for recording their data (Sessions 1 and 2).

▼ Provide materials for presentation graphs and written work, including writing paper, pencils, graph paper of various sizes, markers, stick-on dots, scissors, and construction paper (Session 3).

Important mathematical ideas

Defining a question in data collection.
Defining and discussing the problem is an important first step in data collection and data analysis. Students engage in lively discussions trying to decide what data they need to collect and how to make sense of these data.

Experiencing the phases of data collection and analysis. In doing this project, students experience all the phases of data analysis, as described in the Teacher Note, *Phases of data analysis: Learning from the process approach to writing* (page 65). Working with a real problem, students' analytical skills become sharpened as they investigate the implications of their data collection. Do their chairs fit them? Can they reshuffle them to make them fit? Do they need some different chairs?

Building theories based on data. Using the data they collect, students can develop some theories about human measurements and human growth. They may decide that their chairs do not fit because they have all grown too much or too little; they may find that there are no overall patterns to their chair sizes; they may decide that chairs should be assigned to classrooms based on middle-of-the-year measurements. It is impossible to predict their theories in advance; a teacher's role is to support and probe the students' ideas.

Making presentation graphs and reporting on data analysis activities. This is a chance for your students to review what they have done in the investigation and write about their process and their findings. The opportunity to write and to illustrate that writing is an exciting one for many students. ■

SESSION ACTIVITIES

Children's school desks and chairs are often ill-fitting. Use of furniture tends to evolve over time in a classroom, and children accept what's there without much concern over its fit. Often, more attention is given to the appearance of the chair and desk that a student is to use for the year. Adults' office furniture is taken more seriously. Fitting chairs and desks to people has become an important field of work. Designing chairs, desks, and other parts of a working environment is called *ergonomics*.

Children can be educated to improving the fit of their working furniture. Measuring themselves and the available chairs is a good starting place. In this investigation students determine what dimensions should be taken into account. Do their chairs fit? How can they tell? How could they analyze their body measurements and make some recommendations about chair size? During this project, students will begin to develop their skills at measurement in a problem-solving context that is immediately relevant to them.

Establishing a context for the problem: Goldilocks tries the bears' chairs

Today we're going to start work on a real-life measurement problem. First I want to read you a familiar story to get us started thinking about the problem.

While most third or fourth graders know the story of *Goldilocks*, it is important to reread aloud a version that raises the issue of "fit"—sizes of things vary, and some things fit us while others don't. When you finish reading, allow some time for general response to the story. Then ask students to focus on Goldilocks' feelings of discomfort in the chair that was too big. Did she seem comfortable?

Set three chairs before the class—preferably one that's much too small, one that's about right, and one that's much too big. Ask a very small student to sit in the biggest one. Does it fit? How can people tell by looking? What matches? What doesn't?

Have a large student sit in the smallest chair. You might continue to dramatize the matter of "fit" in a chair until you think your students have some ideas about what dimensions might make a difference.

Defining the problem: How big are we? How big are our chairs?

In the project we're going to do, you will be working in small teams. You'll have the chance to conduct a careful study of your chairs to see whether they are the right size. You'll take careful measurements to see whether the chairs are a good fit. You'll need to talk first about exactly which measurements you'll need, and how the measuring should be done.

Divide the class into small groups of three or four that will work as teams for the duration of the project. Deciding what data to collect in order to evaluate chair sizes will need some serious discussion, either as a whole class or in the small groups that report their decisions back to the whole group. Most students have to work hard to verbalize what they can see. This work is certainly worth the time spent; as they talk, they see how to define the task with more and more precision. For a typical discussion, see the Dialogue Box, *Building a structure for thinking: Does this chair fit?* (page 64). Measuring methods are also an issue: should they measure the front or the back legs of the chairs? The outside or the inside of the human legs? Does it matter? What's the most important dimension: width of the seat? height of the back? height of the seat?

Once students have defined how they will measure the size of the chairs, they will have to decide how to define and measure the crucial dimension of the human leg that determines how a chair fits.

Collecting data: Measuring students and chairs

Students need to collect two pieces of numerical data: the sizes of the chairs and the critical dimension of their fellow students. Decide how they should proceed. You may want the small groups to collect and display the information about the chair sizes in one session and the information about their leg dimensions in another; alternatively, you may want them to collect

both pieces of data in the first session and then graph or display them in another session. In either case, they will need adding machine tape, yardsticks, or tape measures and access to graphing materials. Distribute copies of a class list for students to use to record their data.

Displaying and analyzing data: What sizes do we have?

Working in their small groups to prepare rough draft graphs, students will be looking into two questions: What size chairs do we have available? What size legs do we have? Groups should make a rough draft graph for each kind of data and write one sentence describing the data they have recorded.

When everyone has finished this preliminary analysis, call the class together to look at the ways the information was graphed and to hear each other's comments. Help students focus on the conclusions they are reaching. Do they feel the chair situation is adequate? Do they want to make some recommendations to the school administrators?

Making presentation graphs: Do our chairs fit?

After the class has talked about its conclusions and made some recommendations, the students rejoin their small groups to make final presentation graphs to accompany a written report of their work.

What would the principal need to know about what you've been doing? How could you describe it? What would a letter to the principal sound like?

The production of a final report and accompanying graphs will take the last session of this data analysis project. The important point is that the students draw some conclusions from their work and make some recommendations based on the data they have collected.

Extensions

Some students may want to pursue further the topic of analyzing the design and the size of school furniture. They may want to study another classroom's furniture and see whether those chairs fit the intended users. Or they might study the desk heights in their class and see whether they need or want to make adjustments.

Many third and fourth graders are interested in designing environments. To tap this interest, suggest that they design a school desk and chair (or a working environment) that they would like to use. This could involve measuring their appropriate dimensions and including the measurements in the designs. Or, it might involve a more functional analysis of their needs and their preferences. As a cooperative project, some students might survey the class to learn their preferences, then draw up a report for the designers to use. ■

When ideas are complicated and students seem reluctant or unable to grasp them quickly, teachers have to take an active role in posing problems, clarifying ideas, and helping students figure strategies. It is a very familiar kind of teaching, one that Jerome Bruner calls "scaffolding" children's ideas. Building a structure to support the children's thinking does feel like building a scaffold.

Finding the "right" human dimension to match with the height of a chair is a difficult problem. Students have to isolate one variable from a welter of information. In a situation like this, a teacher has to decide how much scaffolding to provide. In the following dialogue, the teacher is working hard to help students isolate the information they need to know without providing it for them. He is dramatic, energetic, and very active in this process.

We've found that Maria does real well in this chair. What does it have to do with, making the chair fit and you fit in the chair?

SEAN: The body.

What do you mean about the body?

BARBARA: She's small.

She's small. But I could say Ricardo's small, too, but he doesn't fit well in that chair.

[Ricardo sits in Maria's chair. He's too big. Everybody giggles.]

JENNIFER: He doesn't fit.

Why, but why?

BOBBY: He's bigger.

But what does that mean, he's bigger?

KIM: Because his legs and his knees are sticking up.

If I come sit in this chair . . .

KYLE: It's just right.

How do you know it's just right?

MICHAEL: Cause you're big.

But where am I big? You mean my belly? *[Laughter] . . .*

[Later. Now Maria and Ricardo are both sitting in chairs that are too big for them, and the teacher is in a chair that is too small.]

CHRIS: Maria's feet aren't touching the floor, and Ricardo's feet aren't, and yours are.

So, if her feet are off the floor, does it mean the chair is too big or too small?

PEGGY: Too big.

How do we know when your chair is just right?

PEGGY: When your knees are not sticking up.

[Pointing at Maria, whose legs are dangling above the ground] **Her knees are not sticking up. But that's one part.**

BENJAMIN: When it's uncomfortable.

OK. When it's uncomfortable.

SUSAN: When your feet are right on the floor.

My feet are right on the floor, but I'm not comfortable.

TAMARA: The same size. The same size as you.

The same size as what? What should be the same size as what?

☞ In this conversation the teacher pushes the students to clarify, extend, and defend their statements. While he does have an outcome in mind—identifying what parts of the chair and body could be compared and measured in order to determine fit—he repeatedly reflects students' own words and statements back to them and challenges them to take their conjectures further: But what does that mean, he's bigger? How do you know it's just right? What should be the same size as what?

Even when he gets a satisfactory description of what "just right" means ("When your knees are not sticking up"), he does not use that to simplify the complexity of the issue. He accepts the information as important ("That's one part"), but challenges students to think further. This balance between acceptance and questioning provides a scaffold for children's thinking without doing the thinking for them. ∎

Phases of data analysis: Learning from the process approach to writing

The process of data analysis is similar to many other creative processes. Students doing data analysis follow the same processes that adults do; the analyses may be less complex, but the procedures are the same. In data analysis, as in writing or art, teachers help children do real work rather than stilted school assignments requiring fill-in-the-blank responses. The teacher's role is relatively subtle—shaping the process, asking questions that guide the students' progress toward their goals, hearing and responding to their ideas and theories. Students are expected to have something original and interesting to say, and the teacher provides an environment that enriches and supports students' self-expression.

Data analysis has many similarities to the process approach to writing, which typically includes four phases. The process starts with a *planning phase* (often called pre-writing or brainstorming). This is followed by the *writing phase,* when a very rough draft of ideas is first put down on paper. The third phase is the *revision* or *rewriting phase* when the writer elaborates, clarifies, restructures, and edits the piece. The final phase is the *publication phase,* when the writer's completed piece is shared with others. These processes

may be reiterated until the piece of writing is finished.

Data analysis has four phases parallel to those in the writing process:

Phase One: Brainstorming and planning. During this time, students discuss, debate, and think about their research question. In some cases, defining and agreeing upon the question may take a considerable amount of time. Having defined the question and agreed upon terms, students consider possible sources of data, ways of recording them, and how they might organize themselves to collect needed information.

Phase Two: Putting it on paper. For the collection and representation of data, students develop their discovery drafts—what we call "sketch graphs"—the first draft of the information on which they base their developing theories. Students represent the data in a variety of ways to help them describe the important features. They use their first drafts as tools as they look for relationships and patterns in the data.

Phase Three: Revision. Writers are encouraged to share their drafts with their peers in order to determine how an audience perceives their work. Similarly, in the data analysis process, the students often present their sketch graphs, preliminary findings, and beginning theories to their working group in order to see whether their interpretations seem supported by the data, and whether others see things they haven't noticed.

Revision in data analysis may include finding new ways to organize and represent the data, developing better descriptions of the data, collecting additional data, or refining the research questions and collecting a different kind of data.

Phase Four: Publication or display. The nature of "publishing" the results of data analysis varies, just as it does for a story or essay. Sometimes students develop a theory that is the basis for a report on a particular topic; at other times they may develop a theory that inspires further investigation. A completed report of a data analysis investigation may involve a written description of the study with conclusions and recommendations, final presentation graphs of information previously displayed in working graphs, or a verbal or written presentation of the report to an interested audience.

When teachers think about the writing process, their role as facilitator and helper seems familiar and obvious. Of course students need time to think and revise their work! Of course they need to be challenged and led, sensitively, to the next level of awareness. The writing process seems more familiar to most of us than the mathematics process because we, too, have done writing.

The process of data analysis needs the same kind of teacher support. Students need to try their ideas, to rough them out, to be challenged and encouraged to go further in their thinking. It is important that they have time to think and to consider options—and vitally important that they see their work as part of a process. Data analysis, like writing, is not cut and dried. There are many ways to approach a question and many conclusions to be drawn. Like writing, mathematical investigation is a creative blend of precision and imagination. ■

✎ **TEACHER NOTE**
Goldilocks and the three bears

Here is a version of the familiar Goldilocks story for use as an introduction to the investigation, *Do our chairs fit us?**

ONCE UPON A TIME there were three bears who lived together in a house of their own in a wood. Baby Bear was a little, small, wee bear; Mama Bear was a middle-sized bear; and Papa Bear was a great, huge bear. Each of the bears had a porridge pot: a little pot for Baby Bear, a middle-sized pot for Mama Bear, and a great, huge pot for Papa Bear.

*This version was adapted from *The Green Fairy Book*, edited by Andrew Lang (New York: McGraw-Hill, 1966, reprinted from 1892). ■

Each of the bears had a chair to sit in: a little chair for Baby Bear, a middle-sized chair for Mama Bear, and a great, huge chair for Papa Bear. And they each had a bed to sleep in: a little bed for Baby Bear, a middle-sized bed for Mama Bear, and a great, huge bed for Papa Bear.

One day, after they had made the porridge for their breakfast and poured it into their porridge pots, they walked out into the wood while the porridge was cooling, so that they might not burn their mouths by beginning to eat it too soon. And while they were walking, a little girl called Goldilocks came to the house.

First she looked in at the window, and then she peeped in at the keyhole; and, seeing nobody in the house, she opened the door. The door was not fastened, because the bears were good bears who never did anybody any harm, and never suspected that anybody would harm them. So Goldilocks opened the door and went in; and well pleased she was when she saw the porridge on the table. If she had been a thoughtful little girl, she would have waited till the bears came home and then, perhaps, they would have asked her to breakfast; for they were good bears—a little rough, as the manner of bears is, but for all that very good-natured and hospitable. The porridge looked tempting, though, and little Goldilocks set about helping herself.

First she tasted the porridge of Papa Bear,

and that was too hot for her. And then she tasted the porridge of Mama Bear, and that was too cold for her. And then she went to the porridge of Baby Bear and tasted that; and that was neither too hot nor too cold, but just right, and she liked it so well that she ate it up.

Then Goldilocks sat down in the chair of Papa Bear, and that was too tall for her. And then she sat down in the chair of Mama Bear, and that was too big for her. And then she sat down in the chair of Baby Bear, and that was neither too tall nor too big, but just right. So she seated herself in it, and there she sat till the bottom of the chair fell out, and down she went, plop, onto the ground.

Then Goldilocks went upstairs into the bed-chamber. And first she lay down upon the bed of Papa Bear, but that was too high at the head for her. And next she lay down upon the bed of Mama Bear, but that was too high at the foot for her. And then she lay down upon the bed of Baby Bear; and that was neither too high at the head nor at the foot, but just right. So Goldilocks covered herself up comfortably and lay there till she fell fast asleep.

By this time, the three bears thought their porridge would be cool enough; so they had come home to breakfast. Now Goldilocks had left the spoon of Papa Bear standing in his porridge.

"SOMEBODY HAS BEEN AT MY PORRIDGE!"

said Papa Bear in his great, rough, gruff voice.

And when Mama Bear looked, she saw that the spoon was standing in hers, too.

"SOMEBODY HAS BEEN AT MY PORRIDGE!"

said Mama Bear in her middle voice.

Then Baby Bear looked at his, and there was the spoon in the porridge pot, but the porridge was all gone.

"SOMEBODY HAS BEEN AT MY PORRIDGE, AND HAS EATEN IT ALL UP!"

said Baby Bear in his little, small, wee voice.

At this, the three bears, seeing that someone had entered their house and had eaten up Baby Bear's breakfast, began to look about the room. Now Goldilocks had forgotten to put the cushion straight when she rose from the chair of Papa Bear.

"SOMEBODY HAS BEEN SITTING IN MY CHAIR!"

said Papa Bear in his great, rough, gruff voice.

And Goldilocks had flattened down the cushion of the chair of Mama Bear.

"SOMEBODY HAS BEEN SITTING IN MY CHAIR!"

said Mama Bear in her middle voice.

And you know what Goldilocks had done to the third chair.

"SOMEBODY HAS BEEN SITTING IN MY CHAIR, AND HAS SAT THE BOTTOM OUT OF IT!"

said Baby Bear in his little, small, wee voice.

Then the three bears thought it necessary that they should make further search; so they went upstairs into their bedchamber. Now Goldilocks had pulled the pillow of Papa Bear's bed out of its place.

"SOMEBODY HAS BEEN LYING IN MY BED!"

said Papa Bear in his great, rough, gruff voice.

And Goldilocks had pulled the bolster of Mama Bear's bed out of its place.

"SOMEBODY HAS BEEN LYING IN MY BED!"

said Mama Bear in her middle voice.

And when Baby Bear came to look at his bed, here was the bolster in its place; and the pillow in its place upon the bolster; and upon the pillow was the head of Goldilocks—which was not its place at all, for she had no business there.

"SOMEBODY HAS BEEN LYING IN MY BED—AND HERE SHE IS!"

said Baby Bear in his little, small, wee voice.

Goldilocks had heard in her sleep the great,

rough, gruff voice of Papa Bear, and the middle voice of Mama Bear, but only as if she had heard someone speaking in a dream. But when she heard the little, small, wee voice of Baby Bear, it was so sharp and so shrill that it awakened her at once. Up she started; and when she saw the three bears on one side of the bed, she tumbled herself out at the other and ran out the window.

Now the window was open, because the bears, like the good, tidy bears that they were, always opened their bedchamber window when they got up in the morning. Out Goldilocks jumped, and ran through the woods as fast as she could run—never looking behind her. What happened to her afterward I cannot tell you. But the three bears never saw anything more of her again.

HOW CLOSE CAN YOU GET TO A PIGEON?

INVESTIGATION OVERVIEW

What happens

Students experiment to find out how close pigeons (or some other wildlife common in your area, such as squirrels, ducks, or gulls) will let people approach them. First students establish a method and formulate a plan for data collection; then they collect the data; finally they organize and analyze the data and try to draw conclusions about pigeons' "comfort distance" with people. In a final report, students describe how they conducted the investigation and explain their findings.

The activities take three class sessions of about 45 minutes each.

What to plan ahead of time

▼ Have rulers, yardsticks, tape measures, adding machine tape, and pencils available.

▼ Decide whether students will collect data during class or at another time. If a field trip to a nearby park is in order, make the necessary arrangements.

▼ Provide materials for presentation graphs and written work, including writing paper, graph paper of various sizes, markers, stick-on dots, pencils, scissors, and construction paper.

Important mathematical ideas

Defining the question. The first phase in data analysis is defining the question and deciding what data are needed to answer it. Encourage discussion about what the question means: Can we run up to the pigeons? Should we be allowed to feed them?

Finding a workable means of measurement. The question of how to measure distance when the target doesn't hold still is an important one. Students will have lots of ideas about how to measure the distance from themselves to a nervous pigeon, and together the class will define and refine their methods until they have some specific procedures to follow.

Experiencing all the phases of the data analysis process. Data collection, display, and analysis in a sustained investigation like this one is somewhat different from that which took place during the short-term investigations earlier in this unit. See the Teacher Note, *Phases of data analysis: Learning from the process approach to writing* (page 65) for a description of a more extended investigation. Students can explore their questions further because of the additional time; you may find students inspired by this investigation to undertake others. Related issues in their own lives—instances of crowding in the school, or preferences for personal space—may take on importance for some or all of your students.

Building theories based on data. When students understand their data and present it clearly, they can then go on to build theories and to develop stories based on their data. The measuring task in this investigation presents a good opportunity for storytelling and theory-building. Your role is to support and encourage this kind of expression.

Making a report. Many students find writing about a mathematical experience to be very challenging and satisfying. Writing about mathematics needs to be encouraged, since it provides both an avenue for creative expression and a way to express mathematical concepts in "plain language." Some students find it easy to write about presentation graphs; others find it difficult. This should be no different from writing in English class; only the content will be different. The reports or summaries can be fairly short, but should contain thoughtful treatment of both the mathematical content and the interpretation of their data. ■

SESSION ACTIVITIES

The timing of parts of this investigation depends largely on your class and your own needs. Some teachers introduce the investigation and send students out to measure distances after practicing in the classroom. They then split the next two sessions between recording and organizing data and making final presentations based on those data. At the end of the third session, they call everyone together to report about their findings.

Other teachers allow more time for establishing methods and measurement techniques at the start. Because of the need for a final report, they spend one extra session on the final report itself. You will find natural breaks in the activities and can decide your own best pace.

Considering the problem: How close can you get to a pigeon?*

Many animals fly or run away when humans get too close. You've probably noticed that pigeons [or whatever local animal will work for your investigation] let us get a little bit close, but never *very* close. The distance they insist on keeping is called their "comfort distance."

Your challenge for this project is to find out

---

*This problem was suggested by Marilyn Burns in *The I Hate Mathematics! Book* (Boston: Little, Brown, 1975), page 16. It makes a good cooperative project in data collection and analysis.

how close you can get to a pigeon. You will become scientists and conduct an experiment to find out whether there seem to be patterns in the comfort distances of pigeons. First, you will decide what information you need and make decisions about how to collect data. After you go out to collect your data, you'll spend some time back in class putting everyone's data together. From all the data, we'll see whether pigeons seem to follow any patterns about how close they let humans get. Maybe all pigeons have about the same comfort distance. Maybe they vary—we'll find out.

Deciding on a method of data collection: Measuring to a moving target

Ask questions that help students focus on the nature of the task and make decisions about how best to handle it.

How might you collect information about pigeons' comfort distance? What problems might come up? What could you do about them? What tools would you need? Could you do the task alone? How many pigeons should we try this with?

Pick some students to demonstrate the method the class finally settles on. For some ideas, see the Teacher Note, *Measuring your distance from a pigeon: Some ideas* (page 72).

Remind students of the research question they will be addressing with these data: *How close can you get to a pigeon?*

Review with students the method they will be using, reminding them of the importance of everyone's using the same method. Check to see that they have the necessary materials in their groups. Then send students out to do their measuring work or remind them to do this as their mathematics homework assignment.

Sharing stories about data collection: How did it go?

What happened when you measured to see how close you could get to a pigeon?

This investigation leads to some interesting discussion and good stories. Since data collection often produces surprises, let students share their experiences. This will take some time.

Recording data: Getting it all together

Merging these data is important. Students need to put all their data together so that they can think about pigeons as a group. They have enough experience now so that this will be a relatively easy problem to solve. Nevertheless, you need to be sure that all the data are available for everyone to see.

How can we put all these data together so that we can see them all at once? Do you all have the same kind of data? First let's simply list our data on the board so that you can all see whether we have any problems we have to

solve. **Who has some ideas about we can go about that?**

Students decide ways to organizing these data so that they can put them all together to look for patterns. There may be some measurement problems—some groups may have measured in inches, others in feet and inches—and some may not yet have measured their strips of adding machine tape. Have calculators available so that they can convert feet to inches or inches to feet if they need to do so. This is likely to be time-consuming. You may want to allow a 10- or 15-minute work period and then resume tomorrow when all the data are comparable.

Organizing and displaying data: What do our data look like?

Put students into their working teams to make quick sketch graphs that display all the pigeon data. As they make their sketch graphs, encourage them to talk with each other about what they see and to spend some time thinking about what the data show.

Data analysis: Are there patterns in pigeons' comfort distances?

Hold a conversation with the whole class after the teams have made their preliminary observations in small groups. Encourage students to make observations and comments.

What do the data show? Are the results clustered? What was the closest anyone got to the pigeon? What number shows a pigeon that flew away quickly? Look at the range of the data. Is there a lot of difference between pigeons? What might account for some of those differences?

For tips on guiding students through this discussion, review the Teacher Note, *The shape of the data: Clumps, bumps, and holes* (page 22).

Presentation graphs: Building and illustrating theories

What would you say if someone asked you how close you could get to a pigeon? Can you now answer that original question? Is it possible to build theories from these data?

Ask each team to make a presentation graph to illustrate their theory about pigeons' comfort distance and show their results. Have graph-making materials available. Ask each group to write the story of what they found out from these data, illustrating their work with this final presentation graph.

Extensions

In doing this investigation, your students may develop an interest in human comfort distance. They might measure their own comfort distance (the point at which they get uncomfortable with the close presence of another person) and analyze those data. Making classroom furniture arrangements based on these measurements can be a good deal of fun, with some students squished together or sharing desks while others are floating like islands by themselves.

Analyzing the school for crowding can also be useful. Perhaps students can look at the places and times in the school where and when they feel crowded and make recommendations. Cafeteria tables and benches, auditorium seats, and school bus seats could all be sources of data. How closely does their spacing match your students' preferences?

Some fast-food restaurants have tables with stools or chairs attached. Are those distances comfortable for your students? Do they reflect a comfortable distance for conversation while eating? Perhaps your class would like to write to the restaurant to find out how those designs were decided on. A local architect might be able to talk with the class about how human measurement data are useful in his or her work. ■

✎ TEACHER NOTE
Measuring your distance from a pigeon: Some ideas

The comfort distance of an animal depends on the circumstances. Of course, pigeons have more tolerance for other pigeons than they do for people; they also have more tolerance for quiet people than running people. People, too, have comfort distances that vary with the circumstances. Students may want to talk about their own preferences for personal space as a way of understanding the problem of a pigeon's comfort distance.

To measure the tolerance or comfort distance of a pigeon (or another common animal), students have to develop procedures for getting a measurement that is as accurate as possible. One image that sometimes helps in discussing the problem is the shot putter in the Olympics. Because the shot rolls when it is thrown, judges on the field watch for the shot to hit the ground and immediately run over to the place it landed in order to mark it. Your students may have seen this on television.

Using small groups or research teams of three or four students works well for this investigation. In one class, students worked together in threes. One was the pigeon stalker, who walked quietly toward the pigeon and froze when the pigeon took off. Another was the pigeon pointer, who stared at the pigeon,

and, when the pigeon took off, came up to that spot and marked it with a finger. The third was the measurer, who used adding machine tape to mark off the distance from the stalker to the pointer. A fourth student could be a recorder if you need a group of four.

Your students may come up with a very successful method quite different from the one just described. In any case, you will want to have students act out their measurement strategy in class so that they all do the same thing in the field. ■

GIANT STEPS AND BABY STEPS: MEASURING AT HOME

Are you using giant steps or baby steps? _____

Count the steps:

From the stove to the front door. _____

From the kitchen sink to the living room couch. _____

From your bed to the bathroom. _____

From the bathroom to the stove. _____

Measure other distances at home. Write the results here.

From_____ to _____ is _____.

From_____ to _____ is _____.

From_____ to _____ is _____.

From_____ to _____ is _____.

Be sure you label to show giant steps or baby steps!

PACING IN PAIRS

Make an estimate of the number of paces to your target.
Then count how many paces the pacer actually takes.

Caller's name: _____

Pacer's name: _____

Estimate: _____   Estimate: _____

Actual paces: _____   Actual paces: _____

Estimate: _____   Estimate: _____

Actual paces: _____   Actual paces: _____

Estimate: _____   Estimate: _____

Actual paces: _____   Actual paces: _____

Estimate: _____   Estimate: _____

Actual paces: _____   Actual paces: _____

PACING AND TURNING

Write directions for your robot to get to each target.

First target
Forward _____ paces
Turn _____
Forward _____ paces

Second target
Forward _____ paces
Turn _____
Forward _____ paces

Third target
Forward _____ paces
Turn _____
Forward _____ paces

Fourth target
Forward _____ paces
Turn _____
Forward _____ paces

Fifth target
Forward _____ paces
Turn _____
Forward _____ paces

Sixth target
Forward _____ paces
Turn _____
Forward _____ paces

Start at:

End at:

Total number of paces:

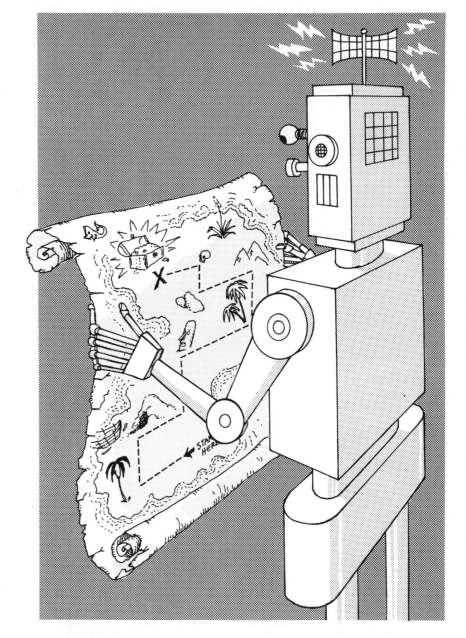

Start at:

End at:

Total number of paces:

Start at:

End at:

Total number of paces:

Start at:

End at:

Total number of paces:

PACING TO DISTANT TARGETS

Write the number of paces and turns
to get to these places in the school.

From our classroom to:

From our classroom to:

From our classroom to:

Total number of paces:

Total number of paces:

Total number of paces:

With your foot ruler, measure the feet of everyone at home. If someone's foot is shorter than the ruler, write the person's name and age in the "shorter" column. If it is longer than the ruler, write the name and age in the "longer" column.

If someone's foot is EXACTLY one foot long, write the name and age in the "equal" column.

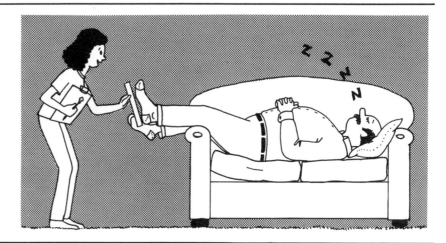

Shorter than the foot ruler		Equal to the foot ruler		Longer than the foot ruler	
Name	Age	Name	Age	Name	Age

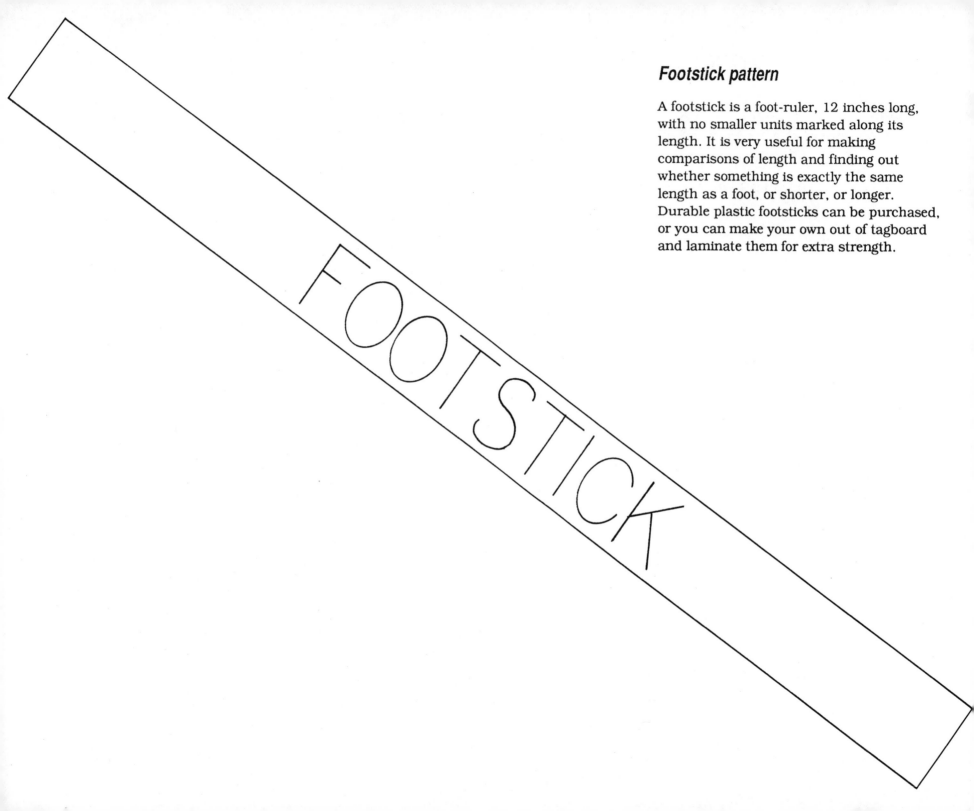

Footstick pattern

A footstick is a foot-ruler, 12 inches long, with no smaller units marked along its length. It is very useful for making comparisons of length and finding out whether something is exactly the same length as a foot, or shorter, or longer. Durable plastic footsticks can be purchased, or you can make your own out of tagboard and laminate them for extra strength.

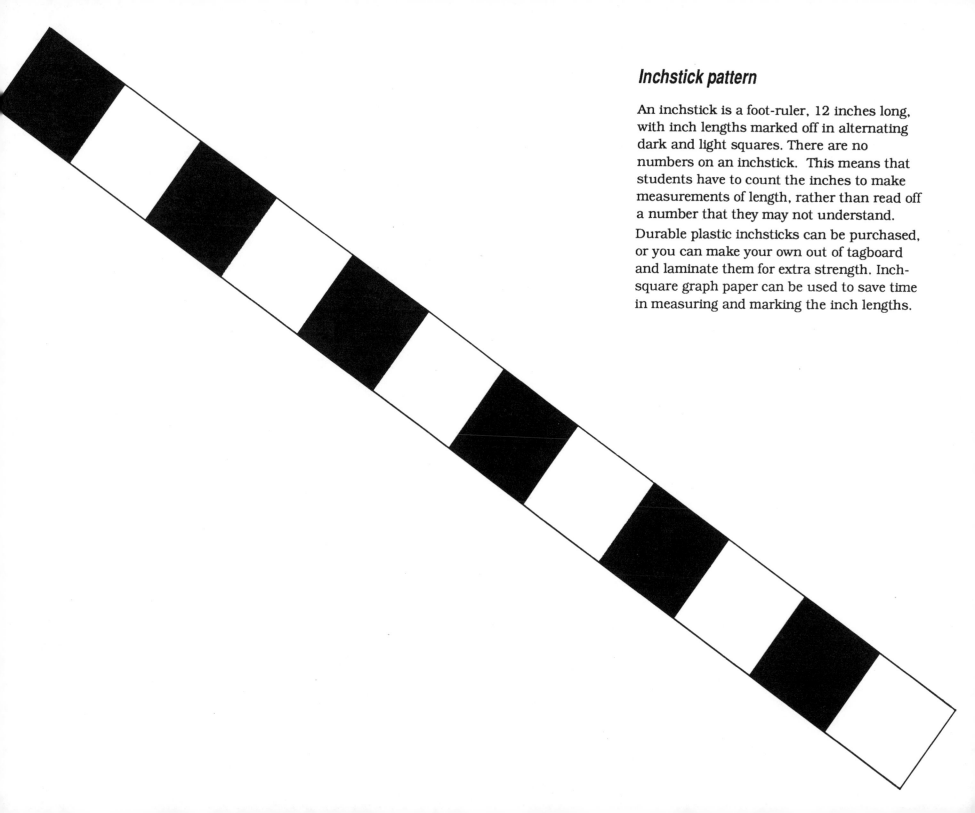

Inchstick pattern

An inchstick is a foot-ruler, 12 inches long, with inch lengths marked off in alternating dark and light squares. There are no numbers on an inchstick. This means that students have to count the inches to make measurements of length, rather than read off a number that they may not understand.

Durable plastic inchsticks can be purchased, or you can make your own out of tagboard and laminate them for extra strength. Inch-square graph paper can be used to save time in measuring and marking the inch lengths.